Modern Critical Interpretations

Franz Kafka's
The Trial

D1218631

Modern Critical Interpretations

These and other titles in preparation

PT
2821
.A26
P75
1987

Modern Critical Interpretations

Franz Kafka's
The Trial

Edited and with an introduction by

Harold Bloom
Sterling Professor of the Humanities
Yale University

LIBRARY
FLORIDA KEYS COMMUNITY COLLEGE
5901 West Junior College Road
Key West, Florida 33040

Chelsea House Publishers ◊ *1987*

NEW YORK ◊ NEW HAVEN ◊ PHILADELPHIA

© 1987 by Chelsea House Publishers,
a division of Chelsea House Educational Communications, Inc.,
 95 Madison Avenue, New York, NY 10016
 345 Whitney Avenue, New Haven, CT 06511
 5014 West Chester Pike, Edgemont, PA 19028

Introduction © 1987 by Harold Bloom

All rights reserved. No part of this publication may be
reproduced or transmitted in any form or by any means
without the written permission of the publisher.

Printed and bound in the United States of America

10 9 8 7 6 5 4 3 2 1

∞ The paper used in this publication meets the minimum
requirements of the American National Standard for
Permanence of Paper for Printed Library Materials,
Z39.48–1984.

Library of Congress Cataloging-in-Publication Data
Franz Kafka's The Trial.
  (Modern critical interpretations)
  Bibliography: p.
  Includes index.
  Summary: A selection of critical essays on Franz Kafka's novel
"The Trial."
  1. Kafka, Franz, 1883–1924. Prozess. [1. Kafka, Franz,
1883–1924.   Trial.   2. German literature—Austrian authors—
History and criticism] I.   Bloom, Harold.   II. Series.
PT2621.A26P75 1987   833′.912   87–9360
ISBN 1-55546-071-2 (alk. paper)

Contents

Editor's Note

This book brings together a representative selection of the best criticism available in English on Franz Kafka's novel *The Trial.* The critical essays and chapters are reprinted here in the chronological order of their original publication. I am grateful to Christina Büchmann for her aid in editing this volume.

My introduction, which seeks to define Kafka's elusive relation to his Jewishness, centers its remarks on *The Trial,* mostly on the parable "Before the Law." Maurice Blanchot begins the chronological sequence of criticism with a vision of Kafka as a writer who "imposed upon himself a minuteness . . . without which a man exiled from reality is rapidly condemned to the errors of confusion." In an analysis of Kafka's language, Heinz Politzer shrewdly notes that "its basic inflection is the cadence of questions."

R. G. Collins finds in Kafka Beckett's precursor, dialectically balancing the tragedy of hope, the comedy of despair. Portraying the enigmas of process in *The Trial,* A. E. Dyson dwells on the pre-Brechtian alienation effect of Kafka's mode of representing Joseph K.

Walter H. Sokel reads *The Trial* as being, like "In the Penal Colony," Kafka's subversion of the mythmaking tendency in his own narrative art. Invoking the genre of the detective story, or mystery and its fictions, David I. Grossvogel expounds the paradox that while Kafka sought to teach us we are in exile from ourselves, his art domesticates us, until we are at home in his narratives.

In this volume's final essay, Martin Walser intimates that Joseph K., like K. in *The Castle,* wears himself out because he encounters no real resistance. The Law is certain of his guilt, and so cannot be bothered with striving against him, but nullifies him instead.

Introduction

In her obituary for her lover, Franz Kafka, Milena Jesenská sketched a modern Gnostic, a writer whose vision was of the *kenoma*, the cosmic emptiness into which we have been thrown:

> He was a hermit, a man of insight who was frightened by life. . . . He saw the world as being full of invisible demons which assail and destroy defenseless man. . . . All his works describe the terror of mysterious misconceptions and guiltless guilt in human beings.

Milena—brilliant, fearless, and loving—may have subtly distorted Kafka's beautifully evasive slidings between normative Jewish and Jewish Gnostic stances. Max Brod, responding to Kafka's now-famous remark—"We are nihilistic thoughts that came into God's head"—explained to his friend the Gnostic notion that the Demiurge had made this world both sinful and evil. "No," Kafka replied, "I believe we are not such a radical relapse of God's, only one of His bad moods. He had a bad day." Playing straight man, the faithful Brod asked if this meant there was hope outside our cosmos. Kafka smiled, and charmingly said: "Plenty of hope—for God—no end of hope—only not for us."

Kafka, despite Gershom Scholem's authoritative attempts to claim him for Jewish Gnosticism, is both more and less than a Gnostic, as we might expect. Yahweh can be saved, and the divine degradation that is fundamental to Gnosticism is not an element in Kafka's world. But we were fashioned out of the clay during one of Yahweh's bad moods; perhaps there was divine dyspepsia, or sultry weather in the garden that Yahweh had planted in the East. Yahweh is hope, and we are hopeless. We are the jackdaws or crows, the kafkas (since that is what the name means, in Czech) whose impossibility is what

1

the heavens signify: "The crows maintain that a single crow could destroy the heavens. Doubtless that is so, but it proves nothing against the heavens, for the heavens signify simply: the impossibility of crows."

In Gnosticism, there is an alien, wholly transcendent God, and the adept, after considerable difficulties, can find the way back to presence and fullness. Gnosticism therefore is a religion of salvation, though the most negative of all such saving visions. Kafkan spirituality offers no hope of salvation, and so is not Gnostic. But Milena Jesenská certainly was right to emphasize the Kafkan terror that is akin to Gnosticism's dread of the *kenoma,* which is the world governed by the Archons. Kafka takes the impossible step beyond Gnosticism, by denying that there is hope for us anywhere at all.

In the aphorisms that Brod rather misleadingly entitled "Reflections on Sin, Pain, Hope and The True Way," Kafka wrote: "What is laid upon us is to accomplish the negative; the positive is already given." How much Kabbalah Kafka knew is not clear. Since he wrote a new Kabbalah, the question of Jewish Gnostic sources can be set aside. Indeed, by what seems a charming oddity (but I would call it yet another instance of Blake's insistence that forms of worship are chosen from poetic tales), our understanding of Kabbalah is Kafkan anyway, since Kafka profoundly influenced Gershom Scholem, and no one will be able to get beyond Scholem's creative or strong misreading of Kabbalah for decades to come. I repeat this point to emphasize its shock value: we read Kabbalah, via Scholem, from a Kafkan perspective, even as we read human personality and its mimetic possibilities by way of Shakespeare's perspectives, since essentially Freud mediates Shakespeare for us, yet relies upon him nevertheless. A Kafkan facticity or contingency now governs our awareness of whatever in Jewish cultural tradition is other than normative.

In his diaries for 1922, Kafka meditated, on January 16, upon "something very like a breakdown," in which it was "impossible to sleep, impossible to stay awake, impossible to endure life, or, more exactly, the course of life." The vessels were breaking for him as his demoniac, writerly inner world and the outer life "split apart, and they do split apart, or at least clash in a fearful manner." Late in the evening, K. arrives at the village, which is deep in snow. The Castle is in front of him, but even the hill upon which it stands is veiled in mist and darkness, and there is not a single light visible to show that the Castle was there. K. stands a long time on a wooden bridge that leads from the main road to the village, while gazing, not at the village, but "into the illusory emptiness above him," where the Castle should be. He does not know what he will always refuse to learn, which is that the emptiness is "illusory" in every possible sense, since he does gaze at the *kenoma,* which resulted initially from the breaking of the vessels, the splitting apart of every world, inner and outer.

Writing the vision of K., Kafka counts the costs of his confirmation, in a passage prophetic of Scholem, but with a difference that Scholem sought to negate by combining Zionism and Kabbalah for himself. Kafka knew better, perhaps only for himself, but perhaps for others as well:

> Second: This pursuit, originating in the midst of men, carries one in a direction away from them. The solitude that for the most part has been forced on me, in part voluntarily sought by me—but what was this if not compulsion too?—is now losing all its ambiguity and approaches its denouement. Where is it leading? The strongest likelihood is that it may lead to madness; there is nothing more to say, the pursuit goes right through me and rends me asunder. Or I can—can I?—manage to keep my feet somewhat and be carried along in the wild pursuit. Where, then, shall I be brought? "Pursuit," indeed, is only a metaphor. I can also say, "assault on the last earthly frontier," an assault, moreover, launched from below, from mankind, and since this too is a metaphor, I can replace it by the metaphor of an assault from above, aimed at me from above.
>
> All such writing is an assault on the frontiers; if Zionism had not intervened, it might easily have developed into a new secret doctrine, a Kabbalah. There are intimations of this. Though of course it would require genius of an unimaginable kind to strike root again in the old centuries, or create the old centuries anew and not spend itself withal, but only then begin to flower forth.

Consider Kafka's three metaphors, which he so knowingly substitutes for one another. The pursuit is of ideas, in that mode of introspection which is Kafka's writing. Yet this metaphor of pursuit is also a piercing "right through me" and a breaking apart of the self.

For "pursuit," Kafka then substitutes mankind's assault, from below, on the last earthly frontier. What is that frontier? It must lie between us and the heavens. Kafka, the crow or jackdaw, by writing, transgresses the frontier and implicitly maintains that he could destroy the heavens. By another substitution, the metaphor changes to "an assault from above, aimed at me from above," the aim simply being the signifying function of the heavens, which is to mean the impossibility of kafkas or crows. The heavens assault Kafka *through his writing*; "all such writing is an assault on the frontiers," and these must now be Kafka's own frontiers. One thinks of Freud's most complex "frontier concept," more complex even than the drive: the bodily ego. The heavens assault Kafka's bodily ego, *but only through his own writing*. Certainly such an assault is not un-Jewish, and has as much to do with normative as with esoteric Jewish tradition.

Yet, according to Kafka, his own writing, were it not for the intervention of Zionism, might easily have developed into a new Kabbalah. How are we to understand that curious statement about Zionism as the blocking agent that prevents Franz Kafka from becoming another Isaac Luria? Kafka darkly and immodestly writes: "There are intimations of this." Our teacher Gershom Scholem governs our interpretation here, of necessity. Those intimations belong to Kafka alone, or perhaps to a select few in his immediate circle. They cannot be conveyed to Jewry, even to its elite, because Zionism has taken the place of Messianic Kabbalah, including presumably the heretical Kabbalah of Nathan of Gaza, prophet of Sabbatai Zvi and of all his followers down to the blasphemous Jacob Frank. Kafka's influence upon Scholem is decisive here, for Kafka already has arrived at Scholem's central thesis of the link between the Kabbalah of Isaac Luria, the Messianism of the Sabbatarians and Frankists, and the political Zionism that gave rebirth to Israel.

Kafka goes on, most remarkably, to disown the idea that he possesses "genius of an unimaginable kind," one that either would strike root again in archaic Judaism, presumably of the esoteric sort, or more astonishingly "create the old centuries anew," which Scholem insisted Kafka had done. But can we speak, as Scholem tried to speak, of the Kabbalah of Franz Kafka? Is there a new secret doctrine in the superb stories and the extraordinary parables and paradoxes, or did not Kafka spend his genius in the act of new creation of the old Jewish centuries? Kafka certainly would have judged himself harshly as one spent withal, rather than as a writer who "only then began to flower forth."

Kafka died only two and a half years after this meditative moment, died, alas, just before his forty-first birthday. Yet as the propounder of a new Kabbalah, he had gone very probably as far as he (or anyone else) could go. No Kabbalah, be it that of Moses de Leon, Isaac Luria, Moses Cordovero, Nathan of Gaza, or Gershom Scholem, is exactly easy to interpret, but Kafka's secret doctrine, if it exists at all, is designedly uninterpretable. My working principle in reading Kafka is to observe that he did everything possible to evade interpretation, which only means that what most needs and demands interpretation in Kafka's writing is its perversely deliberate evasion of interpretation. Erich Heller's formula for getting at this evasion is: "Ambiguity has never been considered an elemental force; it is precisely this in the stories of Franz Kafka." Perhaps, but evasiveness is not the same literary quality as ambiguity.

Evasiveness is purposive; it writes between the lines, to borrow a fine trope from Leo Strauss. What does it mean when a quester for a new Negative, or perhaps rather a revisionist of an old Negative, resorts to the evasion of every possible interpretation as his central topic or theme? Kafka does not doubt guilt, but wishes to make it "possible for men to enjoy sin without guilt, almost without guilt," by reading Kafka. To enjoy sin almost without guilt is to evade interpretation, in exactly the dominant Jewish sense of interpretation. Jewish tradition, whether normative or esoteric, never teaches you to ask Nietzsche's question: "Who is the interpreter, and what power does he seek to gain over the text?" Instead, Jewish tradition asks: "Is the interpreter in the line of those who seek to build a hedge about the Torah in every age?" Kafka's power of evasiveness is not a power over his own text, and it does build a hedge about the Torah in our age. Yet no one before Kafka built up that hedge wholly out of evasiveness, not even Maimonides or Judah Halevi or even Spinoza. Subtlest and most evasive of all writers, Kafka remains the severest and most harassing of the belated sages of what will yet become the Jewish cultural tradition of the future.

II

The jackdaw or crow or Kafka is also the weird figure of the great hunter Gracchus (whose Latin name also means a crow), who is not alive but dead, yet who floats, like one living, on his death-bark forever. When the fussy Burgomaster of Riva knits his brow, asking: "And you have no part in the other world (*das Jenseits*)?", the Hunter replies, with grand defensive irony:

> I am forever on the great stair that leads up to it. On that infinitely wide and spacious stair I clamber about, sometimes up, sometimes down, sometimes on the right, sometimes on the left, always in motion. The Hunter has been turned into a butterfly. Do not laugh.

Like the Burgomaster, we do not laugh. Being a single crow, Gracchus would be enough to destroy the heavens, but he will never get there. Instead, the heavens signify his impossibility, the absence of crows or hunters, and so he has been turned into another butterfly, which is all we can be, from the perspective of the heavens. And we bear no blame for that:

> "I had been glad to live and I was glad to die. Before I stepped aboard, I joyfully flung away my wretched load of ammunition, my knapsack, my hunting rifle that I had always been proud to carry, and I slipped into my winding sheet like a girl into her marriage dress. I lay and waited. Then came the mishap."
>
> "A terrible fate," said the Burgomaster, raising his hand defensively. "And you bear no blame for it?"
>
> "None," said the hunter. "I was a hunter; was there any sin in that? I followed my calling as a hunter in the Black Forest, where there were still wolves in those days. I lay in ambush, shot, hit my mark, flayed the skin from my victims: was there any sin in that? My labors were blessed. 'The Great Hunter of Black Forest' was the name I was given. Was there any sin in that?"
>
> "I am not called upon to decide that," said the Burgomaster, "but to me also there seems to be no sin in such things. But then, whose is the guilt?"
>
> "The boatman's," said the Hunter. "Nobody will read what I say here, no one will come to help me; even if all the people were commanded to help me, every door and window would remain shut, everybody would take to bed and draw the bedclothes over his head, the whole earth would

become an inn for the night. And there is sense in that, for nobody knows of me, and if anyone knew he would not know where I could be found, and if he knew where I could be found, he would not know how to deal with me, he would not know how to help me. The thought of helping me is an illness that has to be cured by taking to one's bed."

How admirable Gracchus is, even when compared to the Homeric heroes! They know, or think they know, that to be alive, however miserable, is preferable to being the foremost among the dead. But Gracchus wished only to be himself, happy to be a hunter when alive, joyful to be a corpse when dead: "I slipped into my winding sheet like a girl into her marriage dress." So long as everything happened in good order, Gracchus was more than content. The guilt must be the boatman's, and may not exceed mere incompetence. Being dead and yet still articulate, Gracchus is beyond help: "The thought of helping me is an illness that has to be cured by taking to one's bed."

When he gives the striking trope of the whole earth closing down like an inn for the night, with the bedclothes drawn over everybody's head, Gracchus renders the judgment: "And there is sense in that." There is sense in that only because in Kafka's world as in Freud's, or in Scholem's, or in any world deeply informed by Jewish memory, there is necessarily sense in everything, total sense, even though Kafka refuses to aid you in getting at or close to it.

But what kind of a world is that, where there is sense in everything, where everything seems to demand interpretation? There can be sense in everything, as J. H. Van den Berg once wrote against Freud's theory of repression, only if everything is already in the past and there never again can be anything wholly new. That is certainly the world of the great normative rabbis of the second century of the Common Era, and consequently it has been the world of most Jews ever since. Torah has been given, Talmud has risen to complement and interpret it, other interpretations in the chain of tradition are freshly forged in each generation, but the limits of Creation and of Revelation are fixed in Jewish memory. There is sense in everything because all sense is present already in the Hebrew Bible, which by definition must be totally intelligible, even if its fullest intelligibility will not shine forth until the Messiah comes.

Gracchus, hunter and jackdaw, is Kafka, pursuer of ideas and jackdaw, and the endless, hopeless voyage of Gracchus is Kafka's passage, only partly through a language not his own, and largely through a life not much his own. Kafka was studying Hebrew intensively while he wrote "The Hunter Gracchus," early in 1917, and I think we may call the voyages of the dead but never-buried Gracchus a trope for Kafka's belated study of his ancestral language. He was still studying Hebrew in the spring of 1923, with his tuberculosis well advanced and down to nearly the end, he longed for Zion, dreaming of recovering his health and firmly grounding his identity by journeying to Palestine. Like Gracchus, he experienced life-in-death, though unlike Gracchus he achieved the release of total death.

"The Hunter Gracchus" as a story or extended parable is not the narrative of a Wandering Jew or Flying Dutchman, because Kafka's trope for his writing activity is not so much a wandering or even a wavering, but rather a repetition, labyrinthine and burrow-building. His writing repeats, not itself, but a Jewish esoteric interpretation of Torah that Kafka himself scarcely knows, or even needs to know. What this interpretation tells Kafka is that there is no written Torah but only an oral one. However, Kafka has no one to tell him what this Oral Torah is. He substitutes his own writing therefore for the Oral Torah not made available to him. He is precisely in the stance of the Hunter Gracchus, who concludes by saying, " 'I am here, more than that I do not know, further than that I cannot go. My ship has no rudder, and it is driven by the wind that blows in the undermost regions of death.' "

III

"What is the Talmud if not a message from the distance?" Kafka wrote to Robert Klopstock, on December 19, 1923. What was all of Jewish tradition, to Kafka, except a message from an endless distance? That is surely part of the burden of the famous parable "An Imperial Message," which concludes with you, the reader, sitting at your window when evening falls and dreaming to yourself the parable—that God, in his act of dying, has sent you an individual message. Heinz Politzer read this as a Nietzschean parable, and so fell into the trap set by the Kafkan evasiveness:

Describing the fate of the parable in a time depleted of metaphysical truths, the imperial message has turned into the subjective fantasy of a dreamer who sits at a window with a view on a darkening world. The only real information imparted by this story is the news of the Emperor's death. This news Kafka took over from Nietzsche.

No, for even though you dream the parable, the parable conveys truth. The Talmud does exist; it really is an Imperial message from the distance. The distance is too great; it cannot reach you; there is hope, but not for you. Nor is it so clear that God is dead. He is always dying, yet always whispers a message into the angel's ear. It is said to you that: "Nobody could fight his way through here even with a message from a dead man," but the Emperor actually does not die in the text of the parable.

Distance is part of Kafka's crucial notion of the Negative, which is not a Hegelian nor a Heideggerian Negative, but is very close to Freud's Negation and also to the Negative imaging carried out by Scholem's Kabbalists. But I want to postpone Kafka's Jewish version of the Negative until later. "The Hunter Gracchus" is an extraordinary text, but it is not wholly characteristic of Kafka at his strongest, at his uncanniest or most sublime.

When he is most himself, Kafka gives us a continuous inventiveness that rivals Dante, and he truly challenges Proust and Joyce as the dominant Western author of our century, setting Freud aside, since Freud ostensibly is science and not narrative or mythmaking, though if you believe that, then you can be persuaded of anything. Kafka's beast fables are rightly celebrated, but his most remarkable fabulistic being is neither animal nor human but is little Odradek, in the curious sketch, less than a page and a half long, "The Cares of a Family Man," where the title might have been translated: "The Sorrows of a Paterfamilias." The family man narrates these five paragraphs, each a dialectical lyric in itself, beginning with one that worries the meaning of the name:

Some say the word Odradek is of Slavonic origin, and try to account for it on that basis. Others again believe it to be of German origin, only influenced by Slavonic. The uncertainty of both interpretations allows one to assume with justice that neither is accurate, especially as neither of them provides an intelligent meaning of the word.

This evasiveness was overcome by the scholar Wilhelm Emrich, who traced the name Odradek to the Czech word *odraditi,* meaning to dissuade anyone from doing anything. Like Edward Gorey's Doubtful Guest, Odradek is uninvited yet will not leave, since implicitly he dissuades you from doing anything about his presence, or rather something about his very uncanniness advises you to let him alone:

> No one, of course, would occupy himself with such studies if there were not a creature called Odradek. At first glance it looks like a flat star-shaped spool for thread, and indeed it does seem to have thread wound upon it; to be sure, they are only old, broken-off bits of thread, knotted and tangled together, of the most varied sorts and colors. But it is not only a spool, for a small wooden crossbar sticks out of the middle of the star, and another small rod is joined to that at a right angle. By means of this latter rod on one side and one of the points of the star on the other, the whole thing can stand upright as if on two legs.

Is Odradek a "thing," as the bemused family man begins by calling him, or is he not a childlike creature, a daemon at home in the world of children? Odradek clearly was made by an inventive and humorous child, rather in the spirit of the making of Adam out of the moistened red clay by the J writer's Yahweh. It is difficult not to read Odradek's creation as a deliberate parody when we are told that "the whole thing can stand upright as if on two legs," and again when the suggestion is ventured that Odradek, like Adam, "once had some sort of intelligible shape and is now only a broken-down remnant." If Odradek is fallen, he is still quite jaunty, and cannot be closely scrutinized, since he "is extraordinarily nimble and can never be laid hold of," like the story in which he appears. Odradek not only advises you not to do anything about him, but in some clear sense he is yet another figure by means of whom Kafka advises you against interpreting Kafka.

One of the loveliest moments in all of Kafka comes when you, the paterfamilias, encounter Odradek leaning directly beneath you against the banisters. Being inclined to speak to him, as you would to a child, you receive a surprise: " 'Well, what's your name?' you ask him. 'Odradek,' he says. 'And where do you live?' 'No fixed abode,' he says and laughs; but it is only the kind of laughter that has no lungs behind it. It sounds rather like the rustling of fallen leaves."

"The 'I' is another," Rimbaud once wrote, adding: "So much the worse for the wood that finds it is a violin." So much the worse for the wood that finds it is Odradek. He laughs at being a vagrant, if only by the bourgeois definition of having "no fixed abode," but the laughter, not being human, is uncanny. And so he provokes the family man to an uncanny reflection, which may be a Kafkan parody of Freud's death drive beyond the pleasure principle:

> I ask myself, to no purpose, what is likely to happen to him? Can he possibly die? Anything that dies has had some kind of aim in life, some kind of activity, which has worn out; but that does not apply to Odradek. Am I to suppose, then, that he will always be rolling down the stairs, with ends of thread trailing after him, right before the feet of my children? He does no harm to anyone that I can see, but the idea that he is likely to survive me I find almost painful.

The aim of life, Freud says, is death, is the return of the organic to the inorganic, supposedly our earlier state of being. Our activity wears out, and so we die because, in an uncanny sense, we wish to die. But Odradek, harmless and charming, is a child's creation, aimless, and so not subject to the death drive. Odradek is immortal, being dae-monic, and he represents also a Freudian return of the repressed, of something repressed in the paterfamilias, something from which the family man is in perpetual flight. Little Odradek is precisely what Freud calls a cognitive return of the repressed, while (even as) a com-plete affective repression is maintained. The family man introjects Odradek intellectually, but totally projects him affectively. Odradek, I now suggest, is best understood as Kafka's synecdoche for *Vernei-nung*; Kafka's version (not altogether un-Freudian) of Jewish Nega-tion, a version I hope to adumbrate in what follows.

IV

Why does Kafka have so unique a spiritual authority? Perhaps the question should be rephrased. What kind of spiritual authority does Kafka have for us, or why are we moved or compelled to read him as one who has such authority? Why invoke the question of authority at all? Literary authority, however we define it, has no necessary relation to spiritual authority, and to speak of a spiritual authority in Jewish writing anyway always has been to speak rather dubiously. Authority is not a Jewish concept but a Roman one, and so makes perfect contemporary sense in the context of the Roman Catholic Church, but little sense in Jewish matters, despite the squalors of Israeli politics and the flaccid pieties of American Jewish nostalgias. There is no authority without hierarchy, and hierarchy is not a very Jewish concept either. We do not want the rabbis, or anyone else, to tell us what or who is or is not Jewish. The masks of the normative conceal not only the eclecticism of Judaism and of Jewish culture, but also the nature of the J writer's Yahweh himself. It is absurd to think of Yahweh as having mere authority. He is no Roman godling who augments human activities, nor a Homeric god helping to constitute an audience for human heroism.

Yahweh is neither a founder nor an onlooker, though sometimes he can be mistaken for either or both. His essential trope is fatherhood rather than foundation, and his interventions are those of a covenanter rather than of a spectator. You cannot found an authority upon him, because his benignity is manifested not through augmentation but through creation. He does not write; he speaks, and he is heard, in time, and what he continues to create by his speaking is *olam,* time without boundaries, which is more than just an augmentation. More of anything else can come through authority, but more life is the blessing itself, and comes, beyond authority, to Abraham, to Jacob, and to David. No more than Yahweh do any of them have mere authority. Yet Kafka certainly does have literary authority, and in a troubled way his literary authority is now spiritual also, particularly in Jewish contexts. I do not think that this is a post-Holocaust phenomenon, though Jewish Gnosticism, oxymoronic as it may or may not be, certainly seems appropriate to our time, to many among us. Literary Gnosticism does not seem to me a time-bound phenomenon, anyway. Kafka's *The Castle,* as Erich Heller has argued, is clearly more Gnostic than normative in its spiritual temper, but then so is Shakespeare's *Macbeth,* and Blake's *The Four Zoas,* and Carlyle's *Sartor Resartus.* We sense a Jewish element in Kafka's apparent Gnosticism, even if we are less prepared than Scholem was to name it as a new Kabbalah. In his 1922 Diaries,

Kafka subtly insinuated that even his espousal of the Negative was dialectical:

> The Negative alone, however strong it may be, cannot suffice, as in my unhappiest moments I believe it can. For if I have gone the tiniest step upward, won any, be it the most dubious kind of security for myself, I then stretch out on my step and wait for the Negative, not to climb up to me, indeed, but to drag me down from it. Hence it is a defensive instinct in me that won't tolerate my having the slightest degree of lasting ease and smashes the marriage bed, for example, even before it has been set up.

What is the Kafkan Negative, whether in this passage or elsewhere? Let us begin by dismissing the Gallic notion that there is anything Hegelian about it, any more than there is anything Hegelian about the Freudian *Verneinung*. Kafka's Negative, unlike Freud's, is uneasily and remotely descended from the ancient tradition of negative theology, and perhaps even from that most negative of ancient theologies, Gnosticism, and yet Kafka, despite his yearnings for transcendence, joins Freud in accepting the ultimate authority of the fact. The given suffers no destruction in Kafka or in Freud, and this given essentially is the way things are, for everyone, and for the Jews in particular. If fact is supreme, then the mediation of the Hegelian Negative becomes an absurdity, and no destructive use of such a Negative is possible, which is to say that Heidegger becomes impossible, and Derrida, who is a strong misreading of Heidegger, becomes quite unnecessary.

The Kafkan Negative most simply is his Judaism, which is to say the spiritual form of Kafka's self-conscious Jewishness, as exemplified in that extraordinary aphorism: "What is laid upon us is to accomplish the negative; the positive is already given." The positive here is the Law, or normative Judaism; the negative is not so much Kafka's new Kabbalah, as it is that which is still laid upon us: the Judaism of the Negative, of the future as it is always rushing towards us.

His best biographer to date, Ernst Pawel, emphasizes Kafka's consciousness "of his identity as a Jew, not in the religious, but in the national sense." Still, Kafka was not a Zionist, and perhaps he longed not so much for Zion as for a Jewish language, be it Yiddish or Hebrew. He could not see that his astonishing stylistic purity in

German was precisely his way of *not* betraying his self-identity as a
Jew. In his final phase, Kafka thought of going to Jerusalem, and
again intensified his study of Hebrew. Had he lived, he would probably have gone to Zion, perfected a vernacular Hebrew, and given us
the bewilderment of Kafkan parables and stories in the language of
the J writer and of Judah Halevi.

V

What calls out for interpretation in Kafka is his refusal to be
interpreted, his evasiveness even in the realm of his own Negative.
Two of his most beautifully enigmatical performances, both late, are
the parable "The Problem of Our Laws" and the story or testament
"Josephine the Singer and the Mouse Folk." Each allows a cognitive
return of Jewish cultural memory, while refusing the affective identification that would make either parable or tale specifically Jewish in
either historical or contemporary identification. "The Problem of
Our Laws" is set as a problem in the parable's first paragraph:

> Our laws are not generally known; they are kept secret by
> the small group of nobles who rule us. We are convinced
> that these ancient laws are scrupulously administered; nev-
> ertheless it is an extremely painful thing to be ruled by
> laws that one does not know. I am not thinking of possible
> discrepancies that may arise in the interpretation of the
> laws, or of the disadvantages involved when only a few
> and not the whole people are allowed to have a say in their
> interpretation. These disadvantages are perhaps of no great
> importance. For the laws are very ancient; their inter-
> pretation has been the work of centuries, and has itself
> doubtless acquired the status of law; and though there is
> still a possible freedom of interpretation left, it has now
> become very restricted. Moreover the nobles have obvi-
> ously no cause to be influenced in their interpretation by
> personal interests inimical to us, for the laws were made to
> the advantage of the nobles from the very beginning, they
> themselves stand above the laws, and that seems to be why
> the laws were entrusted exclusively into their hands. Of
> course, there is wisdom in that—who doubts the wisdom
> of the ancient laws?—but also hardship for us; probably
> that is unavoidable.

In Judaism, the Law is precisely what is generally known, proclaimed, and taught by the normative sages. The Kabbalah was secret doctrine, but increasingly was guarded not by the normative rabbis, but by Gnostic sectaries, Sabbatarians, and Frankists, all of them ideologically descended from Nathan of Gaza, Sabbatai Zvi's prophet. Kafka twists askew the relation between normative and esoteric Judaism, again making a synecdochal representation impossible. It is not the rabbis or normative sages who stand above the Torah but the *minim,* the heretics from Elisha Ben Abuyah through to Jacob Frank, and in some sense, Gershom Scholem as well. To these Jewish Gnostics, as the parable goes on to insinuate: "The Law is whatever the nobles do." So radical a definition tells us "that the tradition is far from complete," and that a kind of Messianic expectation is therefore necessary.

> This view, so comfortless as far as the present is concerned, is lightened only by the belief that a time will eventually come when the tradition and our research into it will jointly reach their conclusion, and as it were gain a breathing space, when everything will have become clear, the law will belong to the people, and the nobility will vanish.

If the parable at this point were to be translated into early Christian terms, then "the nobility" would be the Pharisees, and "the people" would be the Christian believers. But Kafka moves rapidly to stop such a translation: "This is not maintained in any spirit of hatred against the nobility; not at all, and by no one. We are more inclined to hate ourselves, because we have not yet shown ourselves worthy of being entrusted with the laws."

"We" here cannot be either Christians or Jews. Who then are those who "have not yet shown ourselves worthy of being entrusted with the laws"? They would appear to be the crows or jackdaws again, a Kafka or a Hunter Gracchus, wandering about in a state perhaps vulnerable to self-hatred or self-distrust, waiting for a Torah that will not be revealed. Audaciously, Kafka then concludes with overt paradox:

> Actually one can express the problem only in a sort of paradox: Any party that would repudiate not only all belief in the laws, but the nobility as well, would have the whole

people behind it; yet no such party can come into existence, for nobody would dare to repudiate the nobility.
We live on this razor's edge. A writer once summed the
matter up in this way: The sole visible and indubitable law
that is imposed upon us is the nobility, and must we ourselves deprive ourselves of that one law?

Why would no one dare to repudiate the nobility, whether we
read them as normative Pharisees, Jewish Gnostic heresiarchs, or
whatever? Though imposed upon us, the sages *or* the *minim* are the
only visible evidence of law that we have. Who are we then? How is
the parable's final question, whether open or rhetorical, to be answered? "Must we ourselves deprive ourselves of that one law?"
Blake's answer, in *The Marriage of Heaven and Hell,* was: "One Law
for the Lion and the Ox is Oppression." But what is one law for the
crows? Kafka will not tell us whether it is oppression or not.

Josephine the singer also is a crow or Kafka, rather than a mouse,
and the folk may be interpreted as an entire nation of jackdaws. The
spirit of the Negative, dominant if uneasy in "The Problem of Our
Laws," is loosed into a terrible freedom in Kafka's testamentary
story. That is to say: in the parable, the laws could not be Torah,
though that analogue flickered near. But in Josephine's story, the
mouse folk simultaneously are *and* are not the Jewish people, and
Franz Kafka both is *and* is not their curious singer. Cognitively the
identifications are possible, as though returned from forgetfulness,
but affectively they certainly are not, unless we can assume that
crucial aspects making up the identifications have been purposefully,
if other than consciously, forgotten. Josephine's piping *is* Kafka's
story, and yet Kafka's story is hardly Josephine's piping.

Can there be a mode of negation neither conscious nor uncon-
scious, neither Hegelian nor Freudian? Kafka's genius provides one,
exposing many shades between consciousness and the work of repression, many demarcations far ghostlier than we could have imagined without him. Perhaps the ghostliest come at the end of the
story:

Josephine's road, however, must go downhill. The time
will soon come when her last notes sound and die into
silence. She is a small episode in the eternal history of our
people, and the people will get over the loss of her. Not
that it will be easy for us; how can our gatherings take

place in utter silence? Still, were they not silent even when Josephine was present? Was her actual piping notably louder and more alive than the memory of it will be? Was it even in her lifetime more than a simple memory? Was it not rather because Josephine's singing was already past losing in this way that our people in their wisdom prized it so highly?

So perhaps we shall not miss so very much after all, while Josephine, redeemed from the earthly sorrows which to her thinking lay in wait for all chosen spirits, will happily lose herself in the numberless throng of the heroes of our people, and soon, since we are no historians, will rise to the heights of redemption and be forgotten like all her brothers.

"I am a Memory come alive," Kafka wrote in the Diaries. Whether or not he intended it, he was Jewish memory come alive. "Was it even in her lifetime more than a simple memory?" Kafka asks, knowing that he too was past losing. The Jews are no historians, in some sense, because Jewish memory, as Yosef Yerushalmi has demonstrated, is a normative mode and not a historical one. Kafka, if he could have prayed, might have prayed to rise to the heights of redemption and be forgotten like most of his brothers and sisters. But his prayer would not have been answered. When we think of *the* Catholic writer, we think of Dante, who nevertheless had the audacity to enshrine his Beatrice in the hierarchy of Paradise. If we think of *the* Protestant writer, we think of Milton, a party or sect of one, who believed that the soul was mortal, and would be resurrected only in conjunction with the body. Think of *the* Jewish writer, and you must think of Kafka, who evaded his own audacity, and believed nothing, and trusted only in the Covenant of being a writer.

VI

"Guilt" generally seems more a Christian than a Jewish category, even if the guilt of Joseph K. is primarily ignorance of the Law. Certainly Kafka could be judged closer to Freud in *The Trial* than he usually is, since Freudian "guilt" is also hardly distinct from ignorance, not of the Law but of the Reality Principle. Freud insisted that all authority, communal or personal, induced guilt in us, since we share in the murder of the totemic father. Guilt therefore is never to be doubted, but only because we are all of us more or less ill, all plagued by our discomfort with culture. Freudian and Kafkan guilt alike is known only under the sign of negation, rather than as emotion. Joseph K. has no consciousness of having done wrong, but just as Freudian man nurtures the desire to destroy authority or the father, so even Joseph K. has his own unfulfilled wishes against the image of the Law.

The process that Joseph K. undergoes is hopeless, since the Law is essentially a closed Kabbalah; its books are not available to the accused. If traditional questers suffered an ordeal by landscape, Joseph K.'s ordeal is by nearly everything and everyone he encounters. The representatives of the Law, and their camp followers, are so unsavory that Joseph K. seems sympathetic by contrast, yet he is actually a poor fellow in himself, and would be as nasty as the keepers of the Law, if only he could. *The Trial* is a very unpleasant book, and Kafka's own judgment of it may have been spiritually wiser than anything its critics have enunciated. Would there be any process for us to undergo if we were not both lazy and frightened? Nietzsche's motive for metaphor was the desire to be different, the desire to be elsewhere, but Kafka's sense of our motive is that we want to rest, even if just for a moment. The world is our Gnostic catastrophe creation, being broken into existence by the guilt of our repose. Yet this is creation, and can be visibly beautiful, even as the accused are beautiful in the gaze of the camp followers of the Law.

I do not think that the process Joseph K. undergoes can be called "interpretation," which is the judgment of Ernst Pawel, who follows Jewish tradition in supposing that the Law is language. *The Trial*, like the rest of Kafka's writings, is a parable not of interpretation, but of the necessary failure of interpretation. I would surmise that the Law is not all of language, since the language of *The Trial* is ironic enough to suggest that it is not altogether bound to the Law. If *The Trial* has a center, it is in what Kafka thought worthy of publishing: the famous parable "Before the Law." The dialogue concerning the parable between Joseph K. and the prison chaplain who tells it is remarkable, but less crucial than the parable itself:

> Before the Law stands a doorkeeper on guard. To this doorkeeper there comes a man from the country who begs for admittance to the Law. But the doorkeeper says that he

cannot admit the man at the moment. The man, on reflection, asks if he will be allowed, then, to enter later. "It is possible," answers the doorkeeper, "but not at this moment." Since the door leading into the Law stands open as usual and the doorkeeper steps to one side, the man bends down to peer through the entrance. When the doorkeeper sees that, he laughs and says: "If you are so strongly tempted, try to get in without my permission. But note that I am powerful. And I am only the lowest doorkeeper. From hall to hall keepers stand at every door, one more powerful than the other. Even the third of these has an aspect that even I cannot bear to look at." These are difficulties which the man from the country has not expected to meet, the Law, he thinks, should be accessible to every man and at all times, but when he looks more closely at the doorkeeper in his furred robe, with his huge pointed nose and long, thin, Tartar beard, he decides that he had better wait until he gets permission to enter. The doorkeeper gives him a stool and lets him sit down at the side of the door. There he sits waiting for days and years. He makes many attempts to be allowed in and wearies the doorkeeper with his importunity. The doorkeeper often engages him in brief conversation, asking him about his home and about other matters, but the questions are put quite impersonally, as great men put questions, and always conclude with the statement that the man cannot be allowed to enter yet. The man, who has equipped himself with many things for his journey, parts with all he has, however valuable, in the hope of bribing the doorkeeper. The doorkeeper accepts it all, saying, however, as he takes each gift: "I take this only to keep you from feeling that you have left something undone." During all these long years the man watches the doorkeeper almost incessantly. He forgets about the other doorkeepers, and this one seems to him the only barrier between himself and the Law. In the first years he curses his evil fate aloud; later, as he grows old, he only mutters to himself. He grows childish, and since in his prolonged watch he has learned to know even the fleas in the doorkeeper's fur collar, he begs the very fleas to help him and to persuade the doorkeeper to change his mind. Finally his eyes grow dim and he does not know whether the world is really darkening around him or whether his eyes are only deceiving him. But in the darkness he can now perceive a radiance that streams immortally from the door of the Law. Now his life is drawing to a close. Before he dies, all that he has experienced during the whole time of his sojourn condenses in his mind into one question, which he has never yet put to the doorkeeper. He beckons the doorkeeper, since he can no longer raise his stiffening body. The doorkeeper has to bend far down to hear him, for the difference in size between them has increased very much to the man's disadvantage. "What do you want to know now?" asks the doorkeeper, "you are insatiable." "Everyone strives to attain the Law," answers the man, "how does it come about, then, that in all these years no one has come seeking admittance but me?" The doorkeeper perceives that the man is at the end of his strength and that his hearing is failing, so he bellows in his ear: "No one but you could gain admittance through this door, since this door was intended only for you. I am now going to shut it."

Does he actually perceive a radiance, or are his eyes perhaps still deceiving him? What would admittance to the radiance mean? The Law, I take it, has the same status it has in the later parable "The Problem of Our Laws," where it cannot be Torah, or the Jewish Law, yet Torah flickers uneasily near as a positive analogue to the negation that is playing itself out. Joseph K. then is another jackdaw, another Kafkan crow in a cosmos of crows, waiting for that new Torah that will not be revealed. Does such a waiting allow itself to be represented in or by a novel? No one could judge *The Trial* to be grander as a whole than in its parts, and "Before the Law" bursts out of its narrative shell in the novel. The terrible greatness of Kafka is absolute in the parable but wavering in the novel, too impure a casing for such a fire.

That there should be nothing but a spiritual world, Kafka once wrote, denies us hope but gives us certainty. The certainty would seem to be not so much that a radiance exists, but that all access to it will be barred by petty officials at least countenanced, if not encouraged, by what passes for the radiance itself. This is not paradox, any more than is the Kafkan principle propounded by the priest who narrates "Before the Law": accurate interpretation and misreading cannot altogether exclude one another. Kafka's aesthetic compulsion (can there be such?) in *The Trial* as elsewhere is to write so as to create a necessity, yet also so as to make interpretation impossible, rather than merely difficult.

Kafka's permanent centrality to the post-normative Jewish dilemma achieves one of its monuments in *The Trial*. Gershom Scholem found in Kafka not only the true continuator of the Gnostic Kabbalah of Moses Cordovero, but also the central representative for our time of an even more archaic splendor, the broken radiance of Hebraic revelation. Perhaps Scholem was right, for no other modern Jewish author troubles us with so strong an impression that we are in the presence of what Scholem called: "the strong light of the canonical, of the perfection that destroys."

The Work's Space and Its Demand

Maurice Blanchot

> The consolation of writing, remarkable, mysterious, per-
> haps dangerous, perhaps salutary: it is to leap out of the
> ranks of murderers; it is an observation which is an act
> (*Tat-Beobachtung,* the observation which has become act).
> There is an observation-act to the extent that a higher sort
> of observation is created—higher, not more acute, and the
> higher it is, the more inaccessible it is to the rank and file
> (of murderers), the less it is dependent, the more it follows
> the laws proper to its own movement, the more its road
> climbs, joyfully, incalculably. [January 1922]
> (*The Diaries of Franz Kafka,* Martin Greenberg, ed.)

Here literature is proclaimed as the power which frees, the force that
allays the oppressions of the world "where everything feels throt-
tled"; it is the liberating passage from the first to the third person,
from observation of oneself, which was Kafka's torment, to a higher
observation, rising above mortal reality toward the other world, the
world of freedom.

Why this confidence? One might well wonder. One could answer by reflecting that Kafka belongs to a tradition where the highest
things are expressed in a book which is writing par excellence, a
tradition where the combination, the manipulation of letters has
served as the basis of experiences of ecstasy, and where it is said that
the world of letters, the letters of the alphabet, is the true world of
beatitude. To write is to conjure up spirits, perhaps freeing them

From *The Space of Literature,* translated by Ann Smock. ©1955 by Editions Gallimard,
© 1982 by the University of Nebraska Press. University of Nebraska Press, 1982.

against us, but this danger belongs to the essence of the power that liberates.

However, Kafka's was not a "superstitious" mind; there was in him a cold lucidity which made him say to [Max] Brod, as they left at the end of some Hassidic celebrations, "In fact it was more or less the same as a tribe of savages: gross superstitions." We must not, then, limit ourselves to explanations which, while they may be correct, still do not help us understand why Kafka, so sensitive to the deviation implied in every one of the steps he takes, surrendered with such faith to that essential error which is writing. Nor would it suffice to recall in this connection that ever since his adolescence, he had been extraordinarily sensitive to the influence of artists such as Goethe and Flaubert, whom he was often ready to place above everyone because they placed their art above everything. Probably Kafka never entirely separated himself internally from this conception. But if the passion of art was from the beginning so strong and appeared to him for such a long time to be salutary, this is because, from the start, and by "Father's fault," he found himself cast out of the world, condemned to a solitude for which he had literature, not to blame, but rather to thank—for brightening this solitude, making it fertile, opening it onto another world.

It can be said that his debate with his father pushed the negative aspect of the literary experience into the background for him. Even when he sees that his work requires his ruin, even when, still more grave, he sees the opposition between his work and his marriage, he by no means concludes that there is in this work a fatal power, a voice which decrees "banishment" and condemns to the desert. He does not come to this conclusion, because the world has been lost for him ever since the beginning; real existence has been withdrawn from him, or it was never granted him, and when again he speaks of his exile and of the impossibility of escaping it, he will say, "I have the impression of never having come here at all, but of having been pushed already as a little child and then chained to the spot" (January 24, 1922). Art did not cause him this misfortune: art did not even contribute to it, but on the contrary has shed light upon it—has been the "consciousness of unhappiness," its new dimension.

Art is primarily the consciousness of unhappiness, not its compensation. Kafka's rigor, his fidelity to the work's demand, his fidelity to the demands of grief, spared him that paradise of fictions where so many weak artists whom life has disappointed find satisfaction. Art has for its object neither reveries nor "constructions." But it does not describe truth either. Truth needs neither to be known nor to be described—it cannot even know itself—just as earthly salvation asks not to be discussed or represented, but to be achieved. In this sense there is no place for art: rigorous monism excludes all idols. But, in this same sense, if art is not justified in general, it is at least justified for Kafka alone. For art is linked, precisely as Kafka is, to what is "outside" the world, and it expresses the profundity of this outside bereft of intimacy and of repose—this outside which appears when even with ourselves, even with our death, we no longer have relations of possibility. Art is the consciousness of "this misfortune." It describes the situation of one who has lost himself, who can no longer say "me," who in the same movement has lost the world, the truth of the world, and belongs to exile, to the *time of distress* when, as Hölderlin says, the gods are no longer and are not yet. This does not mean that art affirms another world, at least not if it is true that art has its origin, not in another world, but in the other of all worlds (it is on this point, we now see—but in the notes which represent his religious experience rather than in his work—that Kafka takes or is ready to take the leap which art does not authorize).

Kafka vacillates pathetically. Sometimes he seems to do everything to create for himself a dwelling place among men whose "attractiveness is monstrously strong." He tries to get engaged, he gardens, he practices manual tasks, he thinks about Palestine, he procures lodgings in Prague in order to win not only solitude but the independence of a mature, vigorous man. On this level, the debate with the father remains essential, and all the new notes of the *Diaries* confirm this. They show that Kafka hides nothing from himself of what psychoanalysis could reveal to him. His dependence on his family not only rendered him weak, a stranger to manly tasks (as he himself affirms), but, since this dependence horrifies him, it makes all forms of dependence just as unbearable to him—and, to start with, marriage, which reminds him repulsively of his parents', of the family life from which he would like to free himself but to which he would also like to commit himself, for that is obedience to the law, that is the truth, the truth of the father, which attracts him as much as he resists it, so that "really I stand up before my family, and in its circle I ceaselessly brandish knives to hurt it but at the same time to protect it." "This on the one hand."

But on the other hand he always sees more, and sickness naturally helps him see: that he belongs to the other shore; that, banished, he must not bargain with this banishment; neither must he, as though crushed against its border, remain passively turned toward a reality from which he feels excluded and in which he has never even lived since he is not yet born. This new perspective might be merely that of absolute despair, the nihilistic perspective which is too hastily attributed to him. There is no denying that distress is his element. It is his abode and his "time." But this distress is never without hope. This hope is often only the torment of distress—which does not give hope, but prevents one from getting enough even of despair and determines that "condemned to die, one is also condemned to defend oneself right up to the last"—and perhaps at that point assigned to reverse condemnation into deliverance. In this new perspective, the perspective of distress, it is essential not to turn toward Canaan. The wanderer has the desert for a destination, and it is his approach to the desert which is now the true Promised Land. "Is it out there you are leading me?" Yes, out there. But where is that, out there? It is never in sight; the desert is even less certain than the world; it is never anything but the approach to the desert. And in this land of error one is never "here," but always "far from here." And yet, in this region where the conditions of a real dwelling lack, where one has to live in an incomprehensible separation, (an exclusion from which one is, somehow, excluded, just as one is excluded from oneself)—in this region which is the region of error because in it one does nothing but stray without end, there subsists a tension: the very possibility of erring, of going all the way to the end of error, of nearing its limit, of transforming wayfaring without any goal into the certitude of the goal without any way there.

We know that the story of the landsurveyor represents the most impressive image of this move. From the very beginning, this hero of inflexible obstinacy is described to us as having renounced his world, his home, the life which includes wife and children, forever. Right from the start, then, he is outside salvation, he belongs to exile, that region where not only is he away from home, but away from himself. He is in the outside itself—a realm absolutely bereft of intimacy where beings seem absent and where everything one thinks one grasps slips away. The tragic difficulty of the undertaking is that in this world of exclusion and radical separation, everything is false and inauthentic as soon as one examines it, everything lacks as soon as one seeks support from it, but nevertheless the depth of this absence is always given anew as an indubitable, absolute presence. And the word *absolute,* which means "separated," is in its proper place here. For it is as if separation, experienced in all its rigor, could reverse itself and become the absolutely separated, the absolutely absolute.

This must be put more precisely: Kafka—that exacting mind by no means satisfied with the dilemma of all or nothing which he nevertheless conceives more intransigently than anyone else—hints that in this move outside the true there are certain rules. They are perhaps contradictory and indefensible, but still they authorize a sort of possibility. The first is given in error itself: one must stray and not be indolent as Joseph K. is in *The Trial,* imagining as he does that things are always going to continue and that he is still in the world when, from the first sentence, he is cast out of it. Joseph's fault, similar probably to the one with which Kafka reproached himself at the time he was writing this book, is that he wants to win his trial in the world itself, to which he thinks he still belongs, but where his cold, empty heart, his bachelor bureaucrat's existence, his lack of concern for his family—all character traits which Kafka found in himself—already prevent him from getting a footing. Granted, his indifference yields bit by bit, but that is a result of the trial, just as the beauty which shines in the faces of the accused and makes them attractive to women is the reflection of their own dissolution, of death advancing in them like a truer light.

The trial, the banishment, is no doubt a great misfortune; it is perhaps an incomprehensible injustice or an inexorable punishment. But it is also—to be sure, only to a certain extent (and this is the hero's excuse, the trap he falls into)—a given which it does no good to protest by invoking in hollow speeches some higher justice. On the contrary, one must try to gain from it, according to the rule which Kafka made his own: "You must limit yourself to what you still possess." The trial has at least the advantage of making known to K. what is really the case. It dissipates illusion—the deceptive consolations which, because he had a good job and a few indifferent pleasures, allowed him to believe in his existence, in his existence as a man of the world. But the trial is not, for all that, the truth. It is, on the contrary, a process of error, like everything which is linked to the outside, that "exterior" darkness where one is cast by the force of banishment. The trial is a process where if one hope remains, it is for him who advances, not against the current, in futile opposition, but in the very direction of error.

The landsurveyor is almost entirely free of Joseph K.'s faults. He does not seek to return home. Gone is life in Canaan; effaced is the truth of this world; he scarcely even remembers it in brief, pathetic moments. He is not indolent either, but always on the move, never stopping, almost never getting discouraged, going from failure to failure in a tireless movement which evokes the cold disquietude of the time which affords no rest. Yes, he goes ahead, with an inflexible obstinacy, always in the direction of extreme error, disdaining the village which still has some reality, but wanting the Castle, which perhaps has none, detaching himself from Frieda, who retains some glints of life, to turn toward Olga, sister of Amalia, the doubly excluded, the rejected—Amalia who, still worse, in a fearful decision, voluntarily chose to be so. Everything ought to proceed, then, for the best. But nothing of the sort. For the landsurveyor falls incessantly into the fault which Kafka designates as the gravest: impatience. The impatience at the heart of error is the essential fault, because it misconstrues the very trueness of error which, like a law, requires that one never believe the goal is close or that one is coming nearer to it. One must never have done with the indefinite; one must never grasp—as if it were the immediate, the already present—the profundity of inexhaustible absence.

To be sure, it is inevitable that one should do so, and therein lies the desolating character of such a quest. Whoever is not impatient is indolent. Whoever surrenders to the disquietude of error loses the indifference that would exhaust time. Scarcely having arrived, understanding nothing about this ordeal of exclusion in which he finds himself, K. sets out right away to get quickly to the end. He won't expend any energy on the intermediaries; in their regard he is indolent. This is probably to his credit: doubtless it demonstrates the force of his tense striving towards the absolute. But his aberration is not any the less glaring. It consists in taking for the end what is only an intermediary, a representation befitting his "lights."

Surely we are as deceived as the landsurveyor when we think we recognize in the bureaucratic phantasm the fitting symbol of a superior world. This figure merely befits our impatience. It is the palpable form of the error through which, before the impatient gaze, the inexorable force of the evil infinite is ceaselessly substituted for the absolute. K. always wants to reach the goal before having reached it.

This demand for a premature denouement is the principle of figuration: it engenders the *image,* or, if you will, the idol, and the curse which attaches to it is that which attaches to idolatry. Man wants unity right away; he wants it in separation itself. He represents it to himself, and this representation, the image of unity, immediately reconstitutes the element of dispersion where he loses himself more and more. For the image as such can never be attained, and moreover it hides from him the unity of which it is the image. It separates him from unity by making itself inaccessible and by making unity inaccessible.

Klamm is by no means invisible. The landsurveyor wants to see him, and he sees him. The Castle, supreme goal, is by no means out of sight. As an image, it is constantly at his disposal. Naturally when you look at them closely, these figures are disappointing. The Castle is only a cluster of village huts; Klamm, a big heavy man seated in front of a desk. There is nothing here that isn't very ordinary and ugly. But this is the landsurveyor's good luck—the truth, the deceptive honesty of these images: they are not seductive in themselves, they possess nothing to justify the fascinated interest people take in them. Thus they remind us that they are not the true goal. In this insignificance, however, the other truth lets itself be forgotten. And the other truth is that these images are, all the same, images of the goal; they partake of its glow, of its ineffable value, and not to attach oneself to them is already to turn away from the essential.

We could summarize this situation as follows: it is impatience which makes the goal inaccessible by substituting for it the proximity of an intermediary figure. It is impatience that destroys the way toward the goal by preventing us from recognizing in the intermediary the figure of the immediate.

We must limit ourselves here to these few indications. The bureaucratic phantasm, all the bustling idleness which characterizes it, and those double beings who are its functionaries, guards, aides, messengers, who always go two by two as if to show clearly that they are only each other's reflections and the reflection of an invisible whole; moreover, that whole chain of metamorphoses, that methodical enlarging of the distance which is never defined as infinite but necessarily expands indefinitely through the transformation of the goal into obstacles, but also of obstacles into intermediaries leading to the goal—all this powerful imagery does not represent the truth of a superior world, or even its transcendence. It represents, rather, the

favorable and unfavorable nature of figuration—the bind in which
the man of exile is caught, obliged as he is to make out of error a
means of reaching truth and out of what deceives him indefinitely the
ultimate possibility of grasping the infinite.

To what extent was Kafka aware of the analogy between this
move outside truth and the movement by which the work tends
toward its origin—toward that center which is the only place the
work can be achieved, in the search for which it is realized and
which, once reached, makes the work impossible? To what extent
did he connect the ordeal of his heroes with the way in which he
himself, through art, was trying to make his way toward the work
and, through the work, toward something true? Did he often think
of Goethe's words, "It is by postulating the impossible that the
writer procures for himself all of the possible"? This much at least is
strikingly evident: the fault which he punished in K. is also the one
with which the artist reproaches himself. Impatience is this fault. It
wants to hurry the story toward its denouement before the story has
developed in all its directions, exhausted the measure of time which
is in it, lifted the indefinite to a true totality where every inauthentic
movement, every partially false image can be transformed into an
unshakable certitude. This is an impossible task, a task which, if it
were accomplished fully, would destroy that very truth toward which
it tends, just as the work is wrecked if it touches the point which is
its origin. Many considerations restrain Kafka from finishing almost
any of his "stories" and cause him, when he has scarcely begun one,
to leave it in search of peace in another. He states that he often feels
the torment of the artist exiled from his work at the moment it
affirms itself and closes up. He also says that he sometimes abandons
a story in anguish lest, if he didn't abandon it, he could never come
back toward the world, but it is not certain that this concern was in
his case the strongest. That he often abandons a story because every
denouement bears in itself the happiness of a definitive truth which
he hasn't the right to accept, to which his existence does not yet
correspond—this reason also appears to have played a considerable
role. But all these hesitations can be summarized as follows: Kafka,
perhaps without knowing it, felt deeply that to write is to surrender
to the incessant; and, out of anxiety—fear of impatience—and scru-
pulous attention to the work's demand, he most often denied himself
the leap which alone permits finishing, the insouciant and happy

confidence by which (momentarily) a limit is placed upon the interminable.

What has so inappropriately been called his realism reveals this same instinctive effort to exorcise the impatience within him. Kafka often showed that his genius was a prompt, a ready one; he was capable of reaching the essential in a few swift strokes. But more and more he imposed upon himself a minuteness, a slow approach, a detailed precision (even in the description of his own dreams), without which a man exiled from reality is rapidly condemned to the errors of confusion and the approximations of the imaginary. The more one is lost outside, in the strangeness and insecurity of this loss, the more one must appeal to the spirit of rigor, scruple, exactitude; the more one must concentrate on absence through a multitude of images, through their determined and modest appearance—modest because disengaged from fascination—and through their energetically sustained coherence. Anyone who belongs to reality can forego all these details which, as we know, in no way correspond to the form of a real vision. But he who belongs to the depths of the limitless and the remote, to the distress of the immeasurable, yes, that person is condemned to an excess of measure and to strive for continuity without a single misstep, without any missing links, without the slightest inconsistency. And condemned is the right word. For if patience, exactitude, and cold mastery are qualities indispensable for not getting lost when nothing subsists that one could hold onto, patience, exactitude, and cold mastery are also faults which, dividing difficulties and stretching them out indefinitely, may well retard the shipwreck, but surely retard deliverance, by ceaselessly transforming the infinite into the indefinite. In the same way it is measure which, in the work, prevents the limitless from ever being achieved.

Franz Kafka's Language

Heinz Politzer

As can be seen from the few and strangely austere poems he wrote, Franz Kafka was rarely attracted to the sensuous charm of musical language and was not particularly gifted as a lyrical poet. Wladimir Weidlé has ascribed an "almost Mozartian" quality to his prose. Although we share the French critic's admiration for the "incomparable calmness and clarity" of Kafka's diction, we fail to discover in it any trace of Mozart's measured harmony. The beauty of Kafka's style is due to architectural rather than musical qualities. His prose consists primarily of sentences of great latitude, symmetrically organized with phrase following phrase inevitably and tortuously, moving along in seemingly unending circles until the whole edifice is broken off suddenly, indicating further heights which cannot be reached any more. The tower of Babel is indeed one of Kafka's favorite images.

Kafka, like his heroes, was a visual rather than an auditive type. References to music are scarce in his personal documents, and it is hard to imagine him playing a musical instrument or attending a musical performance of a calibre higher than the *cafés chantants* he used to frequent in his earlier days. When, in 1911, he was persuaded to attend a choral concert, he had to confess afterwards, "The effect music has on me is to surround me with a wall, and its only constant influence on me is that, confined in this way, I am different from what I am when free." One wonders how so sagacious a critic as

From *Modern Fiction Studies* 8, no. 1 (Spring 1962). © 1962 by the Purdue Research Foundation, West Lafayette, Indiana.

Rudolf Kassner could maintain that "Kafka, like all chiliasts, was an auditive type. . . . Only an auditive type could have conceived *The Castle*." In the first place, Kafka did not foresee the millennium; what he visualized was his own end. And this he portrayed in images taken from the visible world rather than from the sphere of sounds.

When music is heard in his books, it almost exclusively signifies the invisible, and serves as a symbol of the perennially unattainable, the ineffable, and the unknowable. From the "unknown nourishment" which the insect craves in *The Metamorphosis* while it listens to his sister's violin playing, to the "clear, piercing, continuous note which came without variation literally from the remotest distance" to which the "Investigations of a Dog" are devoted, music is for Kafka's characters the sensation of the most unsensuous. It is endowed with metaphysical power: usually it heralds an ultimate judgment, like the trumpets of Doom. (Brass instruments are among Kafka's favorite images.) So as to stress even more strongly the inhuman quality of sound, Kafka often chooses an animal as the performer of or the listener to this kind of music. To be sure, Josephine the Mouse Singer's piping secures her a "heightened redemption" which frequently has been misread as indicating the artist's death and transfiguration. In fact, however, this "heightened redemption" opens to Josephine nothing but a mausoleum of oblivion where she is forgotten in the company of the other heroes of her people. In Kafka music is an image of the unimaginable.

The symbols Kafka takes from the visible world are often distorted and in a threatening way transparent. The Statue of Liberty at the entrance to his *Amerika* does not raise the torch of enlightenment but brandishes the sword of justice. The goddess of justice who appears on Titorelli's painting in *The Trial* has wings on her heels and looks in the end "exactly like a goddess of the Hunt in full cry." The Greek god who appears when K. dreams in *The Castle* squeaks "like a little girl being tickled" and is the symbol of the same secretary who defeats the hero while he is sleeping. Reality and suprareality interpenetrate these images; one has ceased to be the mirror of the other. Gregor Samsa is not *like* an insect, he *is* one and yet he *is* also human. On the other hand, the tale of Josephine and her Mouse Folk could be called a human story if the writer had not informed us in the title that he intended to lead us into the realm of an animal fable.

Through his language Kafka is able to span the most disparate spheres of experience. The nonthing Odradek is fully equipped with realistic detail, and so is the fantastic execution machine in "In the Penal Colony." Conversely, an unreal and marionette-like quality informs the most human words and gestures of his heroes. Kafka's every word possesses an unmistakable identity: an identity, however, which can be gained only on the very border of human existence.

All who knew Kafka personally have maintained that he was blessed with the gift of humor. His friend Felix Weltsch has written a book tracing the connection between what he calls Kafka's humor and Kafka's religion (*Religion und Humor im Leben und Werk Franz Kafkas*. Berlin: Herbig, 1957). Max Brod has recorded an incident from which the specific coloration of this humor becomes apparent. "We friends of his," Brod recalls, "laughed quite immoderately when he first let us hear the first chapter of *The Trial*. And he himself laughed so much that there were moments when he could not read any further." We may understand their hilarity better when we realize that this meeting must have taken place close to the outbreak of the first World War. The arrest of Joseph K. hit with the shock of recognition these men who, at least theoretically, were subject to lose their freedom through general conscription. This shock threw them into a heightened awareness of their situation, and they relieved themselves in laughter.

Kafka's humor is generally derived from the extreme lack of humor displayed by his figures. Colliding with their deadly seriousness, the world reveals itself as nonsensical. Kafka's laughter is the nervous reaction to this revelation. To Milena he once wrote: "Sometimes I do not understand how human beings have discovered the notion of 'gaiety'; probably it has just been computed as a contrast to sadness." Sadder than this sadness is the idea that any kind of gaiety could be achieved by the cerebral process of a calculation.

To create images is perhaps the noblest game the human spirit has devised to orient and entertain itself in the passing of time. Of this sublime playfulness there is little left in Franz Kafka's language. His imagination was too profoundly literal to allow his images to assume a metaphorical quality.

In a diary entry of December 6th, 1921, Kafka discusses a sentence he has culled from a letter. The sentence runs: "During this dreary winter I warm myself by it," that is, most probably, the letter. On this statement he comments: "Metaphors are one among many things which make me despair of writing," and adds the following explanation: "Writing lacks independence. It depends on the maid who tends the fire, on the cat warming itself by the stove; it is even dependent on the poor old human being warming himself by the stove. All these are independent activities subject to their own laws; only writing is helpless and cannot live in itself. It is comedy and despair."

Even at this late date, two and a half years before his death, Kafka speaks about literature in the derogatory tones Tonio Kröger had chosen to disparage his Muse twenty years earlier. The hackneyed division between "life" and "spirit" is unearthed again. Here, however, Kafka uses this dichotomy solely to discredit language. As long as a metaphor is intended to establish a link, however tenuous, between life and spirit, it produces in the final analysis a negative effect; it exposes the untruth of literature by comparing it with the actuality of existence. The writer who pretends to warm himself by a letter is convicted of lying when he faces a cat truly warming itself by a real fire. Since literary language cannot avoid operating with some sort of metaphors it is condemned to add one lie to another. It is impossible to speak the truth. "Confession," Kafka says, "and the lie are one and the same. In order to confess one tells lies. One cannot express what one is, for this *is* precisely what one is; one can communicate only what one is not, that is, the lie."

To deal appropriately with the "comedy and despair" of writing, Kafka occasionally uses the simple device of exposing language itself as an instrument of deceit. In *The Trial* the parable "Before the Law" is told to convince Joseph K. that he is deluding himself about the Court. Before the law, the priest explains, stands a doorkeeper who denies entrance to a man from the country. Only in the hour of his death is the man informed by the doorkeeper that the door was intended exclusively for him. In order to learn the lesson of this parable it is necessary for K. to identify himself with the man from the country. One would expect the priest to aid this identification by drawing K.'s attention to his counterpart in the story, the man from the country. The exact opposite comes to pass. Imperceptibly but consistently the narrator deflects K.'s mind from the man and focuses it on the doorkeeper. The doorkeeper is introduced in the first sentence of the story, the man from the country in the second. The former is described in detail, the latter is left a blank. The doorkeeper is mentioned twenty-three times during the very brief narrative, the man only eleven times (in the German original, nine times), and of these only twice by his full title, "the man from the country." The word count betrays the priest's (and the court's) intention to delude K. by the high-frequency of the doorkeeper's appearance in the text. There is a certain justice in K.'s conclusion that the priest's tale has turned "lying into a universal principle." But beyond the priest, the court, and the law, it is language itself that stands exposed as the arch-liar.

Another, more subtle, way to combat the innate mendacity of literary language is to force it to reveal its self-contradiction. A paradox forms the core of the first story Kafka wrote after he had arrived at his own style in the crisis of August 1912. In "The Judgment" the sentence which old Bendemann pronounces against his son runs as follows: "An innocent child, yes, that you were, but still more truly you have been a devilish human being." Innocence and wickedness are not presented here as consecutive stages in Georg's development from child to man; instead, language displays the moral ambiguity of human existence in the simultaneity of a paradox. The verdict which follows the judgment likewise contains a paradox: "I sentence you now," the father says, "to death by drowning." Carrying out this sentence, Georg accepts the double role of executioner and condemned assigned to him by his father. Only the language of the paradox can make his suicide both a murder and a sacrificial death.

The paradox permeates Kafka's style and appears even in his most unexpected turns of phrase. In the third chapter of *Amerika* Karl Rossman has been banished by his uncle and forced to leave the Pollunder mansion. The concluding sentence which sums up Karl's sojourn in New York and the neighboring countryside is the epitome of innocence. Karl, the narrator informs us, "chose a chance direction and set out on his way." However, a choice is an act of deliberate decision and the direct opposite of the phrase "a chance direction," which connotes a surrender to the exigencies of the moment. Choosing "a chance direction," Karl pretends to follow his free will while he moves unwillingly down the path which leads him to his next adventure. This brief paradox replaces a definite motivation which would have seemed to Kafka, the suprarealist, a lie.

A still more economical way to conquer the treacherous nature of language is through word play. Kafka's paradoxes spell out the ambiguities of existence, his subtle plays on words cause them to become transparent. Very early in the novel the lord of *The Castle* is identified as "the Count Westwest." Wilhelm Emrich has observed that "this name could refer to the absolute end, the region of death beyond the sunset, but also the transcendence and the conquest of death." Looking more closely, we can watch Kafka at work with this language. If we assume that "West," like the Hotel Occidental in *Amerika*, signifies decline, then the repetition of this one syllable underscores the impression of decay which K. has received on his arrival before the castle: the crumbling walls, the crows around the tower, the long stretches of darkness, the snow of winter. Yet the negative emphasis provided by this repetition is counteracted by the simple law of logic according to which a double negation results in an affirmation. The West of the West may then indicate the decline of the decline, that is, an ascent. Kafka would thus have alluded to eternal life, would have attempted to say in his opaque way what a more believing soul, a Dean of St. Paul's, John Donne, expressed in the line: "And Death shall be no more; Death, thou shalt die." Yet Kafka does not present us with a choice between these two alternatives. He confronts us with the paradox which embraces both. The name "Westwest" is intended to mean both being and nonbeing, eternal life and eternal death, everything and nothing.

This ambivalence becomes apparent when K. receives a decree of appointment from this castle. The signature on the document is illegible. Beside it, however, is stamped the sender's official rank: Chief of Department Roman Ten. This "Department Number Ten" is simultaneously the "Unknown Department," since Roman Ten is identical with a capital "X" which stands for an undefined quantity in German as it does in English. K. is at liberty to replace this "X" with any figure he chooses, but none of his calculations will ever fit without a remainder. Half letter, half number, this "X" is certainly the most concentrated paradox ever devised by Kafka. As such it holds the secret of the castle as well as of its master. The fight upon which K. embarks is an attack on the completely undefinable. It is also a struggle of letters, of "K" versus "X," a Cabalist venture.

The word Cabalist has haunted Kafka criticism ever since Charles Neider used it to describe Max Brod and other theological interpreters. Each school of critics has taken it up to decry the activities of the others and camouflage their own. While engaged in such Cabalistic techniques, they have generally overlooked that the texts at hand treat language very much in the way the original Cabalists used it in telling their stories. I do not know a more appropriate description of

Kafka's imagery than the following: "A hidden and inexpressible reality finds its expression in the symbol. If the symbol is thus also a sign or representation it is nevertheless more than that: . . . a reflection of the true transcendence. The symbol 'signifies' nothing and communicates nothing, but makes something transparent which is beyond all expression." This definition of a Kafka image is taken from Gershom G. Scholem's investigations into the Gnostic elements of Jewish mysticism, which had become part of the teachings of the Cabala and survived in Kafka's creative imagination.

Sharing in the heritage of his race through the vaguest memories, anticipating its future in the nightmares which beset him, Kafka cannot be said to have followed any particular literary tradition, not even the German one. This may annoy those who are eager to keep their national literature a restricted reservation. On the other hand, it adds the dimension of paradoxical truth to Wilhelm Emrich's observation that "the real *Myth of the Twentieth Century* was written by Franz Kafka."

In a letter to Max Brod dated June 1921, Kafka enumerates the obstacles he encountered in the use of his language. These are "the impossibility of desisting from writing, the impossibility of writing in German, the impossibility of writing differently; one could add a fourth impossibility: the impossibility of writing at all." He carried on in spite of these difficulties and told remarkably illuminating stories while he searched for a way through the twilight which has extended from his day to ours.

What he called the "impossibility of writing" was his reluctance to make a statement in the indicative. Hidden in the conditional, however, some of his aphorisms reflect a glimmer of the light which Kafka knew existed but which was darkened beyond recognition in the world surrounding him. His life would have been easy to live, and his task as a writer simple to accomplish, if he had been an agnostic. He had an eminently analytical mind and saw no reason to believe, and yet he continued to suspend even his disbelief and to inquire why it had become impossible for him to see the light.

Franz Kafka's language does not lend itself to statements; its basic inflection is the cadence of questions. These questions he left open as part of his grand design. His very greatness lies in the endeavor to formulate his questions ever anew although he could not hope that an answer would be given—at least to him.

Kafka's Special Methods of Thinking

R. G. Collins

> *Special Methods of Thinking. Permeated with emotion. Everything feels*
> *itself to be a thought, even the vaguest feelings (Dostoevsky).*
>
> The Diaries of Franz Kafka

To read Franz Kafka is to become a critic. For virtually everyone
who encounters his work, it represents an immediate personal challenge. Only the reader devoid of imagination or incapable of being
moved to response escapes the peculiar rip-tide of Kafka's art, for it
operates upon the reader as a condition of being in which definition
is irrelevant, at least so far as definition is construed as being a series
of precepts or logical conclusions. The writings of Kafka will almost
certainly intensify the beliefs of any one of us who respond to those
writings. Yet, somehow, they apparently do not deny in themselves
the opposite set of beliefs. It is probably not inaccurate to say that
Kafka's writings encompass a peculiar emotional truth that may at
times very well be made up of factual elements that are, as facts,
directly contradictory.

Kafka, then, embraces both me and my enemy. And perhaps he
teaches me to do the same, not philosophically, not by asserting as
statement that either of us is right, but by seeing all conclusive
thoughts as peripheral, by asserting *the condition of being* with all its
crucial questions as the only truth we know. The really important
problem for the critic, then, is to determine how, in deliberately

From *Mosaic* 3, no. 4 (Summer 1970). Special Issue: New Views on Franz Kafka.
© 1970 by the University of Manitoba Press.

evading declarative statement, Kafka manages to make an assertion. It is, I think, through an organic concept of art, through an instinctively realized and effectively executed sense of *structure*.

Since Kafka's works are almost all fragments, I obviously do not mean structure in the external sense. Rather, I would identify it as the significant manipulating and juxtaposition of *qualities* of thought, the discovery of "special methods of thinking" made simultaneously in the work by the author and the reader.

If literary structure, seriously regarded, is that complex of converging relationships in a work, then the proper study in Kafka, more perhaps than in any other writer, is not "meaning" but "form." What I refer to as "meaning" here, of course, is that overt or extrapolated declarative content that tells us that a man chooses this way or that way on a question of politics, or morality, or psychology, or ethics, or livestock raising, or anything else.

There is, to be sure, another kind of *meaning*: that which is the total articulation of response to experience, however finally ambiguous it may be as separable statement. This is the territory of Kafka, a world where one thinks one's way through life taking nothing for granted, thinking the way a blind man gropes for objects, carefully feeling and assessing the shape of each encountered element. Ultimately, even ideas become objects of this sort. Everything has, as its primary nature, shape and form which can be, must be, taken wholly seriously (even when comic or absurd), for the great task—fitting them together—is the true task of each man as he rediscovers eternity. Perversely, Kafka's questioning victims are gods creating.

Regarded in any formal sense as a writer of fiction, Kafka was scarcely prolific. As Max Brod laboured his way through the manuscripts, there emerged the three novels—all incomplete—together with a respectable number of short stories—many of which are obviously fragments. Also, and it is one of the few things upon which most Kafka critics have agreed, his stories seem to reflect a fairly limited area of concern. Yet, over his slender corpse, the critics have gathered in croaking flocks, each to snatch at a different morsel. But he has already fed a couple of generations of literary carnivores; astonishingly, the flesh remains intact; each new arrival sees a whole being before him and delightedly assures himself that Kafka was not, in fact, ever really discovered by anyone else before. If Kafka was generally ambiguous, he is personally relevant in a total sense. He was, in every one of his situations, myself—which means that he was never you, who are not myself. Or so he seems to each of us.

The paradox that obsesses Kafka, and which he so hated but made such beautifully effective use of, thus continues to play around him long after his death, like a mischievous ghost that nonetheless tells the truth. Because of his truth in the guise of ambiguity, Kafka is in the position, imposed or otherwise, of having in his writings woven symbolical structures that are universal in the most flexible way; his literary structures are, if I may borrow a phrase from Hildegard Platzer, something like a pair of elastic stockings. They fit any limb upon which they are drawn, containing and defining, while they nonetheless remain external. In effect, any arbitrary interpretation assumes that the only proper shape of the elastic stocking is that revealed as it is worn by the particular critic. As time has passed, of course, more and more critics have observed that such works as *The Trial* or *The Castle* have a comprehensive potentiality that cannot be contained, properly, by narrow interpretation. Which is, simply enough, just another way of saying that the stocking actually is elastic. However, one should not assume, therefore, that it is really shapeless, for that is equal to saying that it is devoid of meaning.

It is not enough to know that the thread is ambiguity; what one has to do with Kafka's work is to determine the nature of the elasticity, the fabric of which it is made. Part of the critical problem is that Kafka will reveal very little that can be absolutely defined within a work. He avoids almost completely any precise statement of meaning; rather than build up a series of meaningful metaphors—a condition vital, for example, to the Freudian critic—Kafka has made the entire work a vast metaphor. This means that everything contributes to the overall image, nothing is important solely for itself, nothing is irrelevant. Every incident, every sentence functions as a strand in the overall form which is meaning (the actual incompleteness of the work means only that there are "holes in the stocking," not that it is indeterminate in form). Kafka conceives this so completely that even the style is intrinsic to that total meaning.

The work on which Kafka's reputation stands most firmly is *The Trial*; while chapters are missing, the work seems to have an ending and a progressive character that satisfies most readers. If any of his work represents mature artistry, it is this novel. Written a few years after *Amerika, The Trial* reveals a style characteristic of what we have come to identify as that of Kafka. Surprisingly, considering the ambiguity invariably associated with Kafka, that style appears to be extremely simple in almost every respect. Compared with, say, Joyce or Rilke, Kafka forms sentences that seem perfectly plain, almost sparse in their directness. On occasion, sentences may be stretched to considerable length, but they are never complicated; in this sense, Faulkner and Kafka represent antitheses to each other. Each phrase is simply stated, each description is decisively drawn, everything is clear—except, of course, the "meaning." More basically, the individual phrases are almost free of metaphors, and Kafka seems to avoid *equivalent* expressions always.

Kafka once wrote, in a diary entry, that metaphors were one of the many things that made him despair in his writing; and his works clearly reflect this attitude. Where most literary artists have a distrust of precise words to *express* meaning, preferring to create the *nature* of their particular reality, Kafka seems to go even further and carefully avoid all referents of meaning. To describe one object in terms of another—perhaps the most common device in literary art—would be to explain meaning indirectly and so place that additional limitation upon it. In part, then, it is the very preciseness and simplicity of Kafka's phrasing that accounts for ambiguity. One is reminded of the literal responses of a child who refuses to answer in generalizations. Each detail represents a meaningless stop; every situation must be broken down into a great number of questions, each trivial in its way, and the total of literal, limited responses finally assessed by the observer for ultimate meaning. To return to an earlier comparison, the blind man's groping, carried over to thought processes.

As a foil to this surface simplicity, Kafka at the same time suggests by an unusual focus and emphasis at certain points that more is implied than has been stated. Each of the apparently trivial elements is in fact an important link and must be regarded as such. The reader is literally forced into a sharp concentration, as though he had been seized by the neck and brought to his knees. As the sentences combine, one realizes, without knowing what it is, that much more is involved than the phrase would suggest in isolation. One need not be consciously aware of it, but in reading Kafka one is no longer allowed to engage in the more or less passive relationship of reader to text that is characteristic of more traditional pieces of writing. The common use of language is direct expression; apparently that is not enough for meaning as Kafka wishes it *to exist*. The mind of the reader cannot be allowed to sit passively in a theatre while meaning is paraded on the stage. Rather, words become catalysts, and the mind of the reader is drawn into the situation of the art in an active sense.

If Kafka had followed the conventional technique of using descriptive terms to display meaning, it would of course be much easier for us. Yet, given what I believe to be Kafka's aim, there is danger in that. When a reader immediately associates each phrase, he knows what the artist means—or, more exactly, he *believes* he knows. However, what Kafka has *created* is, in part, the ambiguous nature of human experience. If the reader were to know—or feel that he knew— specific meaning, the *actual* meaning would be denied and this aspect of truth—ambiguity—would have escaped the reader. In brief, the technique and the meaning are fused.

For this reason, too, while the incidents of such a story as *The Trial* are simple and there are many minute descriptions of attitude and reasoning, there are very few words that sum them up. Within the novel itself, meaningful conclusions at particular points are almost impossible; one must look at the whole, finally.

One might well ask, at this point, whether there is any evidence from Kafka himself to validate this view. The *Diaries* show that his employing of stylistic technique to produce a total meaning of this sort was by no means a matter of chance. In December 1914, while Kafka was working on the manuscript of *The Trial,* he wrote:

> The beginning of every story is ridiculous at first. . . .
> However, one should not forget that the story, if it has any justification to exist, bears its complete organization within itself even before it has been fully formed.

To use Mark Schorer's now labored phrase, technique becomes discovery. We can go farther and say—technique becomes meaning. The working out of the parts that make up the whole is what gives the ultimate form, value, meaning, identity of the art—all fused as one thing.

It is interesting to note, in this connection, that Kafka apparently never accepted an immediate result in *anything* when he could avoid it. Whether in life or in art, this would be a short-circuiting of the meaning to be achieved by the working out of the parts. Consider, for example, this diary entry of October 30, 1911, as it reveals Kafka's strong compulsion to evade "pure" impression by introducing modifying elements:

It is an old habit of mine, at the point when an impression
has reached its greatest degree of purity, whether of joy or
pain, not to allow it to run its salutary course through all
my being, but rather to dispel and cloud its purity by new,
unexpected, weak impressions.

Such a reference taken by itself would not be particularly indicative; however, it is a characteristic alluded to again and again. Two
years later, for example, Kafka was writing: "This fear of something
definite is ridiculous. These are constructions that even in the imagination, where they are alone sovereign, only approach the living
surface but then are always suddenly driven under."

Of all modern writers, no one more than Kafka has had his
incidental writings—diaries, notebooks, letters, etc.—accepted into
the canon of his art. Moreover, if one is going to use incidents from
Kafka's life to assess his work—and no author has had his romances
and family relationships more closely scanned—there seems to be no
reason for not relating these attitudes towards the style which Kafka
uses in his novels: the constant evasion of precise meaning at any one
point. It is clear that Kafka simply did not *believe in* a world of
definite characteristics and principles. One has only to recall any
scene from *The Trial* to see this belief in operation. The elaborate
discussions of possibility by the lawyer Huld or the artist Titorelli are
only the more obvious examples. This, Kafka seems to say, is the
nature of life, and his own life apparently both generated and verified
this belief. His own uncertainties, such as his inability to go through
with marriage despite being engaged three different times, his lack of
confidence in almost every important situation that he encountered;
this aspect of Kafka has been adequately discussed in relation to his
father, and his consciousness of his alienation as a Jew. However,
equally significant in all probability and far less often noted are certain influences of a less emotional kind.

First of all, we ought to recall in passing at least Kafka's own
legal training. He held the doctor's degree in law, the result of de-
voting many hours in his late adolescence and early manhood to the
reading of law texts which were essentially concerned with the different interpretations possible in any single case, and the error potential in immediately passing judgment on anything. That Kafka
did not practice law later does not negate the probable influence of
this training upon him.

More significant, however, is a point readily verifiable by anyone who looks over the early entries in the *Diaries*: the way in which Kafka taught himself the writing craft. The total number of fragments of stories entered in the *Diaries* between 1910 and 1913 is quite large, deceptively large, in fact, for there are only a few *different* stories. Kafka seems to have preferred to write variant versions of an initial situation, developing as many different possibilities as he could (a striking example of this practice are the multiple entries, in 1910, that begin with a reference to the harm done to him by his education). Even at this early point, Kafka regarded a situation as an *object* with a disguised form that had to be looked at from every possible point of view; he implies that writing is a means of analyzing the elements of an experience and a definite decision of any sort can be made only after every test has been applied, every alternative answer considered. The effect of this early habit is clearly visible in his mature works.

The *Diaries* reveal other influences of a less immediate but perhaps more obviously relevant kind. One of the fullest descriptions of a casual acquaintance that Kafka recorded is of a certain "Dr. K." with whom he apparently spent the evening of October 12, 1911, deep in conversation. The description is interesting for its direct relationship to the theme of *The Trial* in that Kafka's friend is mentioned as having proved through exhaustive logic that "the law" must always be in conflict with itself. However, the description also suggests considerable influence on Kafka's style at a time when he had not yet written any of the three novels or any of the major stories. Dr. K., we are told, was extremely talkative; this characteristic so impressed Kafka that he analyzed quite closely the man's mode of conversation. The most significant thing is the participation which is forced upon the listener.

> There are associations with every story, and indeed several, he surveys them all because he has experienced them, must in haste and out of consideration for me suppress many. Some I also destroy by asking questions but remind him by these of others, show him thereby that he is also in control deep into my own thinking.

This analysis suggests two things: first, that if we combine the speaker and the listener, as Kafka refers to them here, we arrive at the precise mode of development used by Kafka in a work such as *The Trial*;

second, that the presentation of a story is realized as being peculiarly effective when the listener (reader) becomes an intimate part of it, associating and completing meaning by his participation. At the end of the description of Dr. K., Kafka observes:

> He is a very good storyteller, by the way, in his stories the detailed expansiveness of the brief is mixed with the vivacious speech that one finds in such [as Dr. K.]. . . . Legal expressions give the speech steadiness, paragraphs are numbered to a high count that seems to banish them into a distance. Each story is developed from its very beginning, speech and counterspeech are produced and, as it were, shuffled up by personal asides, matters that are beside the point, that no one would think of, are first mentioned, then called beside the point and set aside ('A man, his name is beside the point'), the listener is personally drawn in, questioned, while alongside the plot of the story thickens, sometimes preliminary to a story which cannot interest him at all, the listener is even questioned, uselessly of course, in order to establish some kind of provisional connection, the listener's interjected remarks are not immediately introduced, which would be annoying, but are shortly put in the right place as the story goes on, so that the listener is flattered and drawn into the story and given a special right to be a listener. [Punctuation as given— RGC.]

So thorough an analysis and so pointed an understanding directs us to the importance of this entry in the development of Kafka's style, even if we did not have the evidence of very early stories in which Kafka's style is quite different. Certainly one can say that while *The Trial* has much in common with the technique of storytelling that Kafka analyzes here, a very early story such as "Description of a Struggle" (1903)—which has an approximately typical Kafka theme—does not display anything like the same technique. In the same connection, in examining the published *Diaries* (1910–1923), one finds that almost all of what might be called references to style or technique appear in the first years. In retrospect, it seems that Kafka was thinking out his writing techniques at the very time that he observed so minutely the "style" of Dr. K.

It is interesting to compare Kafka's reaction to another talkative friend, just a month later (November 1911). "N." also used repetition to an extreme degree but with him it is not at all creative in function. Kafka found the experience a boring one because N. "produces it again in its old form almost without additions, but also almost without omissions." The repetition remains solely repetition because, as Kafka says, it is "a communication which is not intended to be anything else and is therefore done with when it is finished." Not only was Kafka becoming increasingly conscious of the value of exploring a single idea from every side, he sensed the necessity for enriching the understanding with each return to the idea.

Careful reading of the *Diaries* provides us, further, with some idea as to what Kafka saw as the way to accomplish that, the way style was to convey meaning. In December of 1911 (just a month after he wrote the references last quoted above), Kafka wrote in his diary a fairly long observation on national literature, one of the relatively few times when he recorded an objective literary judgment. Kafka does not talk about literature much in his diaries, of course, and his conclusions on the particular subject are not of great significance, but some of his incidental points are provocative.

One aphoristic comment, not developed beyond the bare statement, reads: "A literature not penetrated by a great talent has no gap through which the irrelevant might force its way." The double negative may make this momentarily confusing, but after that moment the statement is clear enough, even if the extended meaning is not. The paradox that Kafka expresses here is partially clarified, however, a few pages later in the same entry. Speaking of mediocre literature, he comments: "What in great literature goes on down below, constituting a not indispensable cellar of the structure, here takes place in the full light of day." Apparently, the mediocre work deals with an immediate relevance, that which is made up of obvious associations. The great work of art may use this as a foundation, or it may dispense with it, but this obvious relevance does not represent its true value, its ultimate meaning. Finally, of course, the "irrelevant" which only a great talent makes use of does have a unique relevance—this is the nature of the paradox—but one must have the genius to make it function. It is "the hidden relevance of the irrelevant," with which a great talent concerns itself. When one recalls the great mass of what on any obvious level of relationship appears to be "irrelevant" in Kafka's own work, and yet to carry compulsively urgent meanings, it seems clear that he tried consciously to follow that paradox as a definite principle himself.

So far a number of things have been suggested on the basis of coincidence between Kafka's work and ideas expressed by him in other connections. It is, of course, a tenuous association in one sense. However, other factors speak for its probability. The time element, in particular, seems to represent a supporting vote. Only two days after expressing his paradox of the irrelevant, on December 27, 1911, Kafka specifically disavowed the truly irrelevant, the purely capricious, in the following criticism: "An incoherent assumption is thrust like a board between the actual feeling and the metaphor of the description." The vital necessity for *meaning,* as such, is certainly implied, particularly since the statement just quoted occurs as part of a negative final judgment upon a preceding exercise of his own writing. Moreover, the actual correlation between meaningfulness and the apparently irrelevant was firmly established as one of his own characteristics three days later (December 30, 1911) when Kafka wrote the following lines, among the most revealing in his *Diaries,* so far as technique is concerned. The italics are added:

> I cannot imitate at all, I have always failed when I attempted it, it is contrary to my nature. On the other hand, I have a decided urge to imitate them *in their details,* the way certain people manipulate walking sticks, the way they hold their hands, the movements of their fingers, and I can do it without any effort. But this very effortlessness, this thirst for imitation, sets me apart from the actor, because this effortlessness reflects itself in the fact that no one is aware that I am imitating. Only my own satisfied, or more often reluctant, appreciation shows me that I have been successful. *Far beyond this external imitation, however, goes the inner, which is often so striking and strong that there is no room at all within me to observe and verify it, and it first confronts me in my memory.* But here the imitation is so complete and replaces my own self with so immediate a suddenness that, even assuming it could be made visible at all, it would be unbearable on the stage.

As was often true for Kafka, thoughts sparked by something else—in this case, acting—fit equally well the task of writing upon which he was just beginning. During the last month or two of 1911, he was pondering the direction of his art and every other consideration became grist for that mill. Consciously or otherwise, in this period he settled on the technique which he would refine into his greater works. Prior to this date Kafka had produced little of importance, although he was already in his twenty-ninth year and had been writing for almost a decade. In contrast, in the year that would begin just twenty-four hours after he wrote the above diary passage describing "inner motivation," he would start his first novel (*Amerika*) and complete his first major short story ("The Judgment"). If for no other reason, then, the entry of December 30, 1911, on the surface an almost casual discussion of what constitutes a bad actor, is charged with significance.

While Kafka painfully labored over exercises in writing, and left many fragmentary specimens of his fiction in the *Diaries,* he rarely thought out explicitly, at least on paper, his critical theories of writing. He probably did not even stop to sum them up consciously himself. Actually, his external concern with art, particularly up to about the age of thirty, was largely centered on the drama, and the influence of the stage upon him was a considerable one. Of course, in speaking of drama, he talked about art as he himself was to pursue it. While he wrote only one play, the atmosphere of the stage animates his works. The very difference between his art and that of traditional drama is isolated in the quotation given a moment ago, as is the link between them. When he says that he cannot imitate at all, that he has always failed when he attempted it, he is clearly speaking of the *external* representation of life—this point is established when he opposes to it what he calls *inner imitation.* External imitation is the obvious pattern of action in any situation; it is the pattern that the actor attempts to master (according to Kafka) just as it is the material of a completely realistic literature. Yet, certain elements of external action—what Kafka identifies as the way a person may manipulate his walking stick or the way he moves his fingers—these things fascinated Kafka and he felt that he captured such details truthfully. Not the logical pattern, then, but the realistic *detail in itself* represents the effective key. The external insignificance of such trivial elements disguises the art involved; one is not immediately aware of what is being conveyed. However, Kafka himself is well aware of it, which suggests that no such element in his own writing can safely be regarded as capricious.

The real truth of the artistic presentation, however, is that of *inner imitation*. Kafka's description of this quality is important, for it is probably the most significant comment possible upon his work: "the inner, which is often so striking and strong that there is no room at all within me to observe and verify it, and it first confronts me in my memory." One's first reaction in reading this passage is to associate it with automatic writing. There is even some limited value in so doing, but at the same time it must be accompanied by a recognition that while the character of the imitation is not perceived as it is created, it must have an *intrinsic* logic, a truth so deep-seated that it far exceeds that of the logically patterned external imitation. In short, so far as ultimate meaning is concerned, Kafka himself suggests that he may be guided by a valid intuition rather than a conscious design in writing his works. Yet it is a valid intuition; the meaning is there, and he himself perceived it once technique discovered it, once the creation was accomplished.

By rare good fortune, we have proof of this characteristic in operation in Kafka's work, and it is impressive proof since it is associated with one of the most ambiguous passages in *The Trial*—the parable of the doorkeeper told by the priest in the cathedral chapter. In a diary entry written early in 1915, when he was working on *The Trial*, Kafka describes the reading of the manuscript to F. B., the young woman from Berlin to whom he was then engaged. Undoubtedly because of the emotional *impasse* in their relationship, she had been listening without apparent interest:

> During the reading of the doorkeeper story, greater attention and good observation. *The significance of the story dawned upon me for the first time*; she grasped it rightly too, then of course we barged into it with coarse remarks; I began it. (Italics added—RGC.)

This account of the manuscript reading gives us a striking illustration of what Kafka meant when he said that the inner imitation could not be observed as it took place, that it first confronted him in his memory.

The particular force of those external details that Kafka used as the material for meaning remains somewhat ambiguous still (and probably properly so, according to Kafka's view). In general, however, one may say that they are made up of the involuntary, the secondary physical characteristics that define a person *most* intimately because they are the *least* conscious. Kafka's fascination with physical mannerisms is much greater than is his interest in objective description of a person's appearance, or in what a person alleges to believe. Time after time Kafka painstakingly recorded such physical impressions of people who were talking to him, lecturers to whom he was listening, or actors performing on the stage; yet only on rare occasion does he bother noting down what the person has had to say. An example is an account of a reading by his friend Löwy. After mentioning the titles Löwy was reading from, Kafka goes on:

> A recurrent widening of the eyes, natural to the actor, which are then left so for a while, framed by the arched eyebrows. Complete truth of all the reading; the weak raising of the right arm from the shoulder, the adjusting of the pince-nez that seems borrowed for the occasion, so poorly does it fit the nose, the position under the table of the leg that is stretched out in such a way that the weak joint between the upper and lower parts of the leg is particularly in motion; the crook of the back weak and wretched-looking since the unbroken surface of a back cannot deceive an observer in the way that a face does.

Outside of the fact that one normally would not observe such physical details so precisely, Kafka's impression here becomes interesting for two things. First of all, he summarizes the description in advance as "truth of reading," a phrase that generally might be expected to relate to concepts rather than Löwy's physical peculiarities. Second, he sees the true reality manifested in the curving surface of a back, which "cannot deceive" as a face does. What is suggested is a fusion of simple physical qualities and the inner truth of a thing, a possibility that we find echoed time and again in the novels. What, for instance, is the meaning of the Inspector's constantly rearranging things on the night stand in the interrogation in chapter 1 of *The Trial*? No logical conclusion is ever given, and perhaps it means nothing, yet as Kafka conceives the irrelevant, there is a "truth"—to use his own word—in such involuntary characteristics. By their very inconsequence, deliberately focused upon, attention to such things forces one to reevaluate them, to see them as potentially meaningful. There results a need to discover meaning, perhaps to discover how the irrelevant explains life.

As I began by noting, the nature of Kafka's ambiguity frequently involves what seem to be contradictions; in fact, if it were necessary to define his world, the word "contradiction" would probably be the prevailing one. His protagonists are constantly in the position of finding themselves about to accept a situation only to have it twist away from them and take on a directly opposite character. "The right perception of any matter and a misunderstanding of the same matter do not wholly exclude each other," says the prison chaplain in *The Trial*. Joseph K. will discover that there is every likelihood that a positive result will occur, then a moment later a negative one is seen to be equally as likely. K. in *The Castle* is told by Bürgel that granting of his petition is all but impossible; then, as Bürgel talks on, it becomes clear that Bürgel is really saying that under the circumstances he is helpless *not* to grant K.'s petition. Still later we learn that Bürgel is in no position to grant anything, yet even this is not conclusive since the person saying this really knows no more than K. does.

In part this use of contradiction as the foundation of experience is what makes Kafka's novels seem incapable of ending; they are simply stopped. As is life. It is almost inevitable that they were left in incomplete form, since they assert that nothing can be finally proven. Joseph K. accepts only the necessity of his death, not the validity of it (and even the necessity is thrown into question as the knife descends).

Kafka's use of contradiction seems almost obsessive. Privately, he was repelled by contrary elements. "My repugnance for antitheses is certain," he wrote in 1911; and in using them in his novels as a basic condition of life, he so expressed one of the few precise criticisms that can be traced. He goes on to say of antitheses:

> They are unexpected, but do not surprise, *for they have always been there*; if they were unconscious, it was at the very edge of consciousness. *They make for thoroughness, fulness, completeness, but only like a figure on the "wheel of life"* [an optical toy giving the illusion of a figure in movement]; *we have chased our little idea around the circle.* They are as undifferentiated as they are different, they grow under one's hand as though bloated by water, beginning with the prospect of infinity they always end up in the same medium size. They curl up, cannot be straightened out, are mere clues, are holes in wood, are immobile assaults, draw

antitheses to themselves. If they would only draw all of them, and forever. (Italics added.)

This passage so clearly echoed in all of Kafka's writings is in part verification of the sense of the absurdity of life that Camus saw in Kafka and that Camus himself made a foundation for his own work. Life, which seems to promise infinity, comes to the same thing in the end, no matter what one does. Because everything has its own contradiction within itself, it ultimately reduces life to an optical illusion; our progress towards meaning is nothing but a trick. This aspect of Kafka's belief, expressed in both his stories and his private notes, is one more item in the treatment of his work as mental biography. It has been developed at considerable length by Kafka critics and justifiably so. Yet it is *not* a final answer.

The very nature of Kafka's conception of antithesis, pessimistic as it is from one point of view, necessarily eliminates a final conclusion of pessimism, and Kafka himself did not accept it as final. The end of *The Trial* is death, and there seems never to have been any question of guilt, but this is *the imposed interpretation derived from experience*. Finally all is not seen as beyond redemption, though the point becomes an academic one (as I mentioned earlier, Kafka did have to stop). As Joseph K. is executed, he is still pondering whether something has not been overlooked; a moment before the knife falls, a figure with outstretched arms is perceived in the distance. Is it illusion? Perhaps, but no less or no more than the rest of experience.

The same is true of the other novels. Max Brod, in his Postscript to *The Castle,* maintains that the unwritten end of that novel was to include a partial equivocal acceptance of K. in the village. While *Amerika* is less clear a situation, the last extant chapter, "The Great Nature Circus," is the most optimistic piece of writing that we have from Kafka and certainly suggests a possibility of affirmation despite the author's last comment that "the innocent Rossman" would die. While it would be ridiculous to resurrect Kafka as a resounding voice of hope, it is at the same time not unreasonable to say that his conception of contradiction rendering life absurd was far from a denial of possible value. In fact, the points noted above in connection with the endings of the three novels are firmly supported by Kafka's attitude on that subject in his journals.

As late as 1922, when he was at one of the lowest points in his always precarious health and had not yet found temporary amelioration through the relationship with Dora Diamant, he wrote: "The Negative alone, however strong it may be, cannot suffice, as in my unhappiest moments I believe it can." Man's consciousness may represent guilt, but the nature of guilt does not simply end in an execution.

More truly, the nature of man's dilemma is struggle—this is the contradiction peculiar to it. We are helpless, but we cannot help struggling. Contradiction, paradox, antithesis—all of these terms suggest concepts in conflict. In a way, the title of Kafka's earliest extant work—"Beschreibung eines Kampfes"—is prophetic of the entire body of his writings. As he phrased it on one occasion in those last years of illness, "If I am condemned, then I am not only condemned to die, but also condemned to struggle till I die."

One cannot finally destroy hope. Kafka's literary prototypes refuse to die, as does *The Stranger* of Camus. Even inevitability is a contradiction, which means that there is as much truth in one side of the contradiction as in the other. As long as life remains, says Kafka, hope is an essential part of it. Hope is the affirmative side of Kafka's contradiction; and therefore his contradiction paradoxically suggests a value in life even when its impossibility seems proven. As Kafka advised himself in 1913:

> Don't despair, not even over the fact that you don't despair. Just when everything seems over with, new forces come marching up, and precisely that means that you are alive. And if they don't, then everything is over with here, once and for all.

Such is the importance of the contradiction in life, and such is the use of the endless contradiction employed as device by Kafka in the development of his novels. Not hopelessness but struggle, not defeat but defeat contended against by hope. Contradiction, the technique, as a direct parallel to the essential meaning.

Anticipating Beckett, Kafka sees life as a tragedy of hope, a comedy of despair. He recognizes the great truth of art, its vital tie to instinct—that art dies when it becomes answer, that it bursts into life as it discovers possibility.

Trial by Enigma: Kafka's *The Trial*

A. E. Dyson

Among the many reflections which spring to mind when reading *The Trial,* I find two that predominate: the first, that whatever it may ultimately "mean" it is, for me, one of the most important and relevant books of this century, and the second, that it is curiously similar in some ways to *Alice in Wonderland* and *Through the Looking-Glass.* To start from the second of these points, a simple illustration of the similarity might be found in the following extract:

> On his way up he disturbed many children who were playing on the stairs and looked at him angrily as he strode through their ranks. "If I ever come here again," he told himself, "I must either bring sweets to cajole them with or else a stick to beat them."

The strange and dreamlike quality of the situation (K. has been summoned to his first interrogation, and is searching for the law courts in a block of working-class flats), and the directness and clarity of K.'s logic within the situation, are very reminiscent of Carroll. It may be then that an attempt to compare and contrast Carroll and Kafka will provide one of the many possible approaches that can be made to *The Trial.* This at least will be my hope in what follows.

The undertaking is of course a limited one by its very nature. A large-scale account of Kafka would have, I think, to compare his work with the Book of Job, with *The Divine Comedy,* with *King*

From *Between Two Worlds: Aspects of Literary Form.* © 1972 by A. E. Dyson. Macmillan, 1972.

Lear, and with other major explorations of man's basic religious problems. What is man, what is value, what are the ways and purposes of God? These are the questions Kafka has chiefly in mind, the questions that make him of major importance as a writer, and clearly they transcend anything that Carroll has consciously in mind when writing his books about Alice. The comparison with Carroll is on a more modest scale therefore than comparison with Dante or Shakespeare would be, and it starts from a similarity in technique rather than from similarity of conscious intention. I fancy, however, that a likeness in technique points also to a likeness in sensibility, and that something more important than the remarking of a stylistic coincidence will be found to be in question.

The Alice books are, first and foremost, children's tales, full of charm and delight, and certainly among the best ever written. They cannot therefore be interpreted as books embodying any conscious exploration of religious problems, and upon this most important difference between Carroll and Kafka I want to insist at the start. When it has been allowed for, however, I think we can go on to say that behind the strange logic of Carroll's nonsense, and the archetypal contours of his dream situations, a pattern of *feeling* may be discerned that is not dissimilar to Kafka's. And it is for this reason, I believe, that Alice is not merely a children's heroine, but one who is perpetually fascinating to adult and mature minds as well. In her travels she proves herself, like Joseph K., an eager seeker for understanding in new and baffling territory. Her meetings with strange characters who tell her conflicting stories and are by no means all well disposed towards her are not unlike K.'s various encounters in *The Trial.* Like all children she is disposed to question everything in the search for logical explanations; and, like Joseph K., she finds that logic, far from clarifying and patterning events, serves very often only to make confusion worse confounded. Like Joseph K. also, she is fated always to be questioning her "identity." . . .

Kafka-like overtones are implicit in Alice's situation; and in so far as such overtones are unplanned and therefore committed to no single intended interpretation, they are all the richer in their wide suggestiveness. The strange room in which Alice finds herself, with many doors to choose from on either side, and at the end a small door, impossible to pass through, yielding a view on to the ideal garden beyond, springs to mind at once as an example. The situation is one that symbolises a great many different, and not necessarily consistent ideas—the dangers and difficulties of choice; the insecurity of human experience; the perennial lure of perfection and of the ideal; the vicissitudes of man's emotional search for happiness through the ages, or his intellectual search for truth. Associations such as these are potentially present in such a situation; they are evoked by it, whether with the conscious consent of the author or not. They make their impact on us as we read (a subconscious impact until they are brought to the surface for analysis) and contribute to the sense of significance which a mature mind finds in Carroll's books. They might be called the method in his madness, or the imaginative centre of his effect (*if* to call them this is not to confuse one effect of the books with the actual purpose of their author).

Most of the situations in *Wonderland* and *Through the Looking-Glass* are rich in potential associations of this kind. The caucus race, haphazard, without rules, without beginning or end, culminating in the verdict "Everybody has won, and all must have prizes" (though Alice herself has to give the prizes, since there is no one else to do so); and the croquet match, with its shifting arena, dominated by the arbitrary and terrifying judgements of the Queen of Hearts, ending with the removal of all the players to be executed (though we later hear that they are not really to lose their heads—that is only the Queen's "fancy")—these situations would have suited Kafka. He could have heightened the emotional intensity, used the evocative quality of the situations consciously instead of unconsciously, and imported them into his own pattern of events in *The Trial*.

The trial of the Knave of Hearts, to be more specific, is remarkably like K.'s first interrogation. The atmosphere in the courtroom is similar—a crowd of unfamiliar and curious people, all very conscious of Alice in the one case, K. in the other, all responding unpredictably to what is said, all involved in a complex and inexplicable proceeding. The charge against the Knave of Hearts is shrouded in verbal mystery; the evidence is a chaotic jumble; there is a precarious balance between "important" and "unimportant," so that in the end one does not know which of these terms is the more applicable; there is a call for the sentence before the verdict and the collapse of the court in the end into meaninglessness:

> "Off with her head!" the Queen shouted at the top of her voice. Nobody moved.

> "Who cares for *you*?" said Alice (she had grown to her
> full size by this time). "You're nothing but a pack of cards."

All these things remind us of Kafka; the degree of seriousness is different, but the situation is very like that of K. in *The Trial*.

To list the moments in Carroll when large and often sinister "meanings" suggest themselves would occupy the rest of this chapter. A few will have to be sufficient. Consider for example the difficulties of life in Looking-Glass Land—where an all-out effort is needed not for progress, but merely to avoid losing ground ("it takes all the running *you* can do, to keep in the same place"); where any likelihood of positive rewards is an illusion existing only in the past or future ("Jam to-morrow and jam yesterday—but never jam to-day"); where Humpty Dumpty can state the problem of terminology as devastatingly as the most advanced of Logical Positivists ("When *I* use a word," Humpty Dumpty said, in rather a scornful tone, "it means just what I choose it to mean—neither more nor less"); where the Oriental pessimism of Tweedledum and Tweedledee can identify Alice's whole existence with the insubstantial dreams of the Red King ("Well, it's no use *your* talking about waking him," said Tweedledum, "when you're only one of the things in his dream. You know very well you're not real"); and where Alice can arrive as a Queen at a feast given in her honour, only to be received as a stranger and intruder. All these difficulties about life in Looking-Glass Land at least suggest, in their concrete and profound symbolism, some of the most abiding and disturbing crises in our human lot.

Alice is logical in her questionings, but the dream is too complex, too shifting, too enigmatic, to be plumbed by her logic. She cannot find a system into which it all fits; she cannot cram her Wonderland and Looking-Glass Land into a simple pattern. Bafflement of this kind is the experience also of Joseph K., and is at the core of the comparison I am trying to make. K., like Alice, is in a strange and enigmatic situation; he is tried by enigma, and he cannot understand his experience; he cannot reduce it to a pattern.

In Carroll the overtones of his situations are incidental; in Kafka they are intended, and constitute a religious exploration of reality. The method which Carroll hit upon by accident, and without fully understanding its implications, is used deliberately and with conscious artistry by Kafka. The situations are meant to be meaningful, and their meaning is precisely the impossibility of grasping by logic what the meanings are. As in Carroll, in other words, there is no simple or limiting "interpretation" of the situations in which K. finds himself, no single allegorical intention of the type we find in Bunyan. But whereas in Carroll the overtones are incidental to a pleasant and enthralling tale, in Kafka they are at the very core of what he is doing. They amount to a profound, and profoundly disturbing, vision of human life.

> Someone must have been telling lies about Joseph K., for without having done anything wrong he was arrested one fine morning.

So *The Trial* begins, and we are plunged into the essential mystery. Who has been telling lies, what lies have been told, and why? The unwary reader might suppose that this riddle will be resolved as he reads on, but actually, the clearest statement that he is likely to find has already been made. The situation is presented clearly enough—an arrest, with its problems of who has ordered the arrest, and why, and on what pretext. But the answers to such questions, though K. seeks them single-mindedly and with all his faculties as a man, recede, and blur, and dissolve as he grasps for them. His greatest need is to understand, and this is no mere academic need, it is one on which his very life depends. Though he searches, however with his mind, he discovers only new problems, new difficulty, new levels of enigma. The situation grows around him, absorbs him, moves him further and further away from the everyday world of normality. In that world men may live by convention, think little, and have the illusion, at least, of knowing what they are doing and why they are doing it. But for K. the commonplace world is stripped away. He is torn from the pattern of an ordered society, where familiarity with things is mistaken for understanding of them and security is to be found in an accepted and unquestioned body of convention, and plunged into a position where he finds himself alone and isolated, not knowing the rules, not knowing if there are any rules; life itself at stake, and no "path or friendly clue" to be his guide.

At first, after the arrest, he still thinks in familiar terms—it is a practical joke, a mistake; it can be settled by a few words with an intelligent man, or by the production of some relevant documents. Only gradually does he come to realise how completely the arrest has destroyed the pattern of his past existence, and thrown him into a place where no assumption is safe, no technique works, no person can be trusted, no development can be "placed" or understood. His subsequent attempts to make the universe rational and safe again are all so many types of failure. His sense of insecurity and unreality increases as the unanswerability of fundamental questions becomes clear.

"The thought of his case never left him now." Analysis of the situation turns out, often enough, to be analysis of his relationships with other people, and this, in turn, to be a branch of self-analysis. "To ask questions was surely the main thing." But what questions? That, in itself, is a puzzle. Continuous intellectual activity leading away from, not towards, understanding this state, which the medieval (and Miltonic) world considered to be a prerogative of Lucifer, is the one in which K., as a modern man in search of religious truth, finds himself involved. Moments of clarity, when a logical pattern seems on the point of emerging from the chaos, always lead him on to betrayal. During his first interrogation, for example, he addresses the officials present—and as he does so, emboldened to attack them for injustice, he gathers confidence for a moment from the clichés that start to come.

> There can be no doubt that behind all the actions of this court . . . a great organisation at work. . . . An organisation which . . . employs corrupt warders, stupid inspectors . . . innocent persons accused of guilt . . . innocent men humiliated in the presence of public assemblies.

For a moment the situation is generalised, simplified to the clearly defined formula of innocence as the victim of corruption. K. forgets his own involvement, slips back into the confidence of an everyday frame of reference, takes refuge from reality behind a familiar routine of rhetoric, speaks in the manner of one writing a protest to a daily paper. But, as he speaks, the audience begins to react strangely, he is aware of mounting hostility, he realises that he may have made a fatal miscalculation, the nightmare uncertainty beyond and around his logic reasserts itself. What is he really talking about? What are his premises? Who is he talking to? What is he really doing here? Logic stumbles and breaks against these unanswerable riddles; he is talking in a vacuum, using words that had a meaning once, but have no longer that meaning now. The framework of cliché and stock response, simple hypothesis and simple judgement, has broken up, it has been utterly discredited. There can be no possibility of a return to it.

K.'s uncertainty relates especially to his relationships. Even the most familiar people become bewildering and inaccessible—his landlady, his neighbour, his colleagues at the bank. They speak and act as they used to, but do they mean what they seem to mean? The court officials are at the root of the enigma. K. does not even know whether they are friends or enemies. There is evidence for both views; to commit himself to one of them would be to simplify, not so to commit himself is to risk making the most frightful of errors. They can, he knows, seem to be courteous, conscientious, hard-working. They take pains to explain to him about the "higher powers"; and if their explanations merely increase the number of things that need to be explained, can this be urged against them as their fault? But, on the other hand, their friendliness may be the merest façade. It may be that they have no authority to speak, or are misinformed when they do. Their very offers to help may be only a "cat-and-mouse" game, a diabolical delight in his weakness. "Was the Advocate seeking to comfort him or to drive him to despair? He could not tell."

This insecurity is mirrored in his relationship with Fräulein Bürstner. The situation between them starts simply enough, but almost out of nothing complexities develop, or are assumed to have developed, that defy analysis. K. comes to a point where he is talking in riddles to Fräulein Bürstner's friend, who acts as an intermediary between them—every word making the situation less tangible, and yet the very fact that they are talking about it in such a way establishing the fact that there is a complex situation to be dealt with. "His relationship with Fräulein Bürstner seemed to fluctuate with the case itself." Here, as elsewhere in the book, the image of a labyrinth becomes the controlling one. The mind loses its way, is defeated:

> Things fall apart; the centre cannot hold;
> Mere anarchy is loosed upon the world.

A microcosm of this aspect of the work occurs in the penultimate chapter of the book as we have it, "In the Cathedral." A priest calls K. by name and, having secured his attention, tells him the following parable:

Before the Law stands a door-keeper on guard. To this door-keeper there comes a man from the country who begs for admittance to the Law. But the door-keeper says that he cannot admit the man at the moment. The man, on reflection, asks if he will be allowed, then, to enter later. "It is possible," answers the door-keeper, "but not at this moment." Since the door leading into the Law stands open as usual and the door-keeper steps to one side, the man bends down to peer through the entrance. When the door-keeper sees that, he laughs and says: "If you are so strongly tempted, try to get in without my permission. But note that I am powerful. And I am only the lowest door-keeper. From hall to hall, keepers stand at every door, one more powerful than the other. Even the third of these has an aspect that even I cannot bear to look at." These are difficulties which the man from the country has not expected to meet, the Law, he thinks, should be accessible to every man and at all times, and when he looks more closely at the door-keeper in his furred robe, with his huge pointed nose and long thin, Tartar beard, he decides that he had better wait until he gets permission to enter. The door-keeper gives him a stool and lets him sit down at the side of the door. There he sits waiting for days and years. He makes many attempts to be allowed in and wearies the door-keeper with his importunity. The door-keeper often engages him in brief conversation, asking him about his home and about other matters, but the questions are put quite impersonally, as great men put questions, and always conclude with the statement that the man cannot be allowed to enter yet. The man, who has equipped himself with many things for his journey, parts with all he has, however valuable, in the hope of bribing the door-keeper. The door-keeper accepts it all, saying, however, as he takes each gift: "I take this only to keep you from feeling that you have left something undone." During all these long years the man watches the door-keeper almost incessantly. He forgets about the other door-keepers, and this one seems to him the only barrier between himself and the Law. In the first years he curses his evil fate aloud; later, as he grows old, he only mutters to himself. He grows childish, and since in his prolonged watch he has learned to know even the fleas in the door-keeper's fur collar, he begs the very fleas to help him and to persuade the door-keeper to change his mind. Finally his eyes grow dim and he does not know whether the world is really darkening around him or whether his eyes are only deceiving him. But in the darkness he can now perceive a radiance that streams immortally from the door of the Law. Now his life is drawing to a close. Before he dies, all that he has experienced during the whole time of his sojourn condenses in his mind into one question, which he has never yet put to the door-keeper. He beckons the door-keeper, since he can no longer raise his stiffening body. The door-keeper has to bend far down to hear him, for the difference in size between them has increased very much to the man's disadvantage. "What do you want to know now?" asks the door-keeper, "you are insatiable." "Everyone strives to attain the Law," answers the man, "how does it come about, then, that in all these years no one has come seeking admittance but me?" The door-keeper perceives that the man is at the end of his strength and his hearing is failing, so he bellows in his ear: "No one but you could gain admittance through this door, since this door was intended only for you. I am now going to shut it."

K.'s immediate reaction, as always, is an attempt to analyse the parable. In its literal meaning, it tells the story of one man's search for the truth, including the mysterious answers and glimpses which he seems to have revealed to him, and the apparent ironic injustice of the fate he eventually meets. In its relation to K. as he attempts to understand it, the parable as a whole stands for the data provided to the human mind by its experience of life. It is described by the Priest as "scripture," because every word of it is part of the evidence that the mind has to work on, and nothing therefore can be ignored. K.'s efforts to elucidate the parable's "meaning," like that of other "commentators" whom the Priest mentions, are inspired by a desire for intellectual clarification. He searches for some key principle, some simple explanation of the door-keeper's relationship to the man from the country, which will make sense of everything that happens. Every hypothesis he tries, however, turns out to be incomplete, in that it leaves some aspect of the parable unaccounted for. The function of the Priest, who stands for something not unlike Intellectual Integrity, is to point every time to the aspects of the parable that do not fit in with K.'s hypothesis, and to insist upon the sacredness of "scripture." Anyone, he implies, can formulate some sort of theory, but only a theory covering all the facts is finally of any value, and this is exactly what logic, if K. is ruthlessly honest, cannot provide.

The outlines of the "meaning" of the parable seem clear enough. The man from the country is the human pilgrim, engaged on his search for truth. The door-keeper is in some sense the theory or philosophy or religion which he finds, and accepts as his authority. The result of their encounter is that the man seems in the end to have been betrayed. His life has passed away in waste and unfulfilment, because he is either misinformed of the truth or has misunderstood it; and this because the door-keeper is either deliberately lying, or because he does not have the authority he claims, or because he does represent an authority but the authority is too strange to be understood.

Each time K. proposes a theory, the Priest points out defects in terms of the actual wording of the parable. His technique is that of the fundamentalist interpretation of scripture, but it is turned upon the data of life itself. The Priest insists that his business is not to provide an hypothesis of his own, but to bear constant witness to the evidence.

> I am only showing you the various opinions concerning that point [he tells K. at one stage]. You must not pay too much attention to them. The scriptures are unalterable, and the comments often enough merely express the commentators' bewilderment.

K., defeated in his various attempts to elucidate, drops at last into silence.

> He was too tired to survey all the conclusions arising from the story, and the trains of thought into which it was leading him were unfamiliar, dealing with impalpabilities better suited to a theme for discussion among Court Officials than for him. The simple story had lost its clear outline; he wanted to put it out of his mind.

This exhaustion may well remind us of a similar remark that occurs earlier in *The Trial.*

> You must remember [K. is told] that in these courts things are always coming up for discussion that are simply beyond reason; people are too tired and distracted to think and so they take refuge in superstition.

"Superstition," in this context, seems a term wide enough to cover any dogmatism, any convention, any *Weltanschauung,* however large or internally coherent it might be.

I want now to return to the comparison and contrast with Lewis Carroll, in order to find a centre for these comments.

Right up to the end of the nineteenth century, many moral beliefs remained unchallenged by society at large. The breakdown of traditional faith had gone a long way, Matthew Arnold had heard the sea of faith retreating with a "melancholy, long withdrawing roar," but morality, at least, was much as it was. Indeed, many Victorians imagined that the sterner moral commitments were self-evident, and used them to belabour the religion which had in fact created them and made them prevail. Arnold himself was also clear that the Church of England must at all costs be preserved and continued—modified (of course) in its actual theology, but kept alive as an essential guardian and dispenser of sweetness and light.

Lewis Carroll was near enough to a tradition of intellectual agnosticism to feel that all things had been called in doubt, but not near enough to it perhaps to take the possibility of a complete breakdown of moral and social certainties seriously. He was near enough to it to know all the disturbing questions that could be asked, but not near enough to believe that the questions might end by destroying European civilisation itself. The more anarchic suggestions of, say, Humpty Dumpty concerning "language," or of Tweedledum concerning Alice's "reality" were still, to him, strictly speaking, *nonsense.* They could be played with by his keenly logical mind, and used in the creation of a make-believe world for children, but they were not yet in danger of becoming *sense,* and in so doing, of threatening the very foundations of social sanity and order.

Alice, it will be noticed, is in no ways neurotic; she does not feel guilty, or hunted, or persecuted. Not even the most determined exponents of abnormal psychology could make her anything other than she is, a normal, happy, and essentially delightful little girl. "But I'm *not* a serpent, I tell you," she says to the Pigeon and we have no cause to doubt her. She is sometimes frightened a little, usually perplexed, and even made to cry a little on occasions; but throughout her trial by enigma she never loses her dignity and is always equal to the Queen of Hearts and the other alarming figures she meets. In the end she wakes up to sanity and finds the people of her dreams only a pack of cards after all.

The total feeling of Carroll's books is different, in short, from the feeling of Kafka's. And in view of the similarity of the archetypal patterns in both, this difference seems to me worthy of comment. The adventures which Alice meets with are pleasant adventures, and the characters she meets are basically pleasant characters. Generations of children have found them to be so at any rate, and in this matter no surer critics could be found. The very perplexities that Alice meets with are a source of pleasure to her as she teases her mind with them, and not a cause of pain. In the background of her adventures, also, order rather than chaos is to be discerned. In Looking-Glass Land the order is that appropriate to a game of chess, with something, too, of the feeling of a game of chess—where problems occur, but inside the framework of known rules, and the solving of them is no more than a pleasant academic exercise for the intellect. (Alice herself, of course, does not know the "rules," but Lewis Carroll, her creator, does.) In the last analysis, the Alice books are healthy and sane and satisfying in their effect; the experience of reading them is nothing like the experience of reading Kafka.

All of this may be only another way of saying that Carroll's work is intended for the pleasure of children, and is not in any sense a religious allegory. Nevertheless, in view of their potentially Kafkaesque situations, which could so easily have taken on disquieting overtones had Carroll been less securely rooted in Christian values than he was, a tentative generalisation might perhaps be risked. For Carroll, the topsy-turvy world he created was a welcome escape from the everyday world. Just because the order and sanity of Victorian England was everywhere accepted, he could afford to delight in puzzlement and the reversal of normality as a relief from stern reality. The symbolic situations of Wonderland and Looking-Glass Land were no more than fantasy to him. This is why he was unaware of their potential for real despair.

It is not until we come to our own century, with its fragmentation of culture, its religious and moral doubts, and its final breakdown of any remnants of a *Weltanschauung* that can be said to be generally accepted, that similar symbolic situations turn from charming nonsense to sinister sense.

The situation of K. in *The Trial* is an embodiment of Kafka's own sensitive and troubled search for religious truth. I have said enough to indicate my own high opinion of it, and should like, before making a personal assessment, to defend it against two charges that are often made. The first of these is that K. is not a representative man at all but a neurotic, and that his predicament can be regarded more properly as a department of morbid psychology than as a profound religious allegory. In support of this indictment, it can be pointed out that K. has a decided persecution complex, that he has an unhealthy consciousness of anxiety arising from the circumstances of his arrest, and that his moral and intellectual values diverge further and further as the trial proceeds from those of normal everyday "common sense." He is moreover emotionally unstable, and his moods of elation and despair arise from chance encounters or associations of ideas rather than from any rational causes or coherent trains of thought.

There is of course an element of truth in this; but to conclude on these grounds alone that K. is a neurotic is to ignore the events that happen to him in the book. Unless the extreme view is taken that his "trial" is entirely a subjective fantasy, we have to admit that his feelings of persecution and guilt are not unrelated to an adequate external cause. He would be a psychopathic "case" only if his feelings arose groundlessly. Since they are related to an actual situation, and are by no means psychologically inappropriate to it, there is no evidence for concluding that he is seriously abnormal.

We have cause in our own time to know that ordeals like that to which K. is subjected, and the emotions to which they necessarily give rise, are by no means reserved for the mentally unbalanced. The machinery of ordinary legal proceedings, and of ordinary bureaucratic proceedings, are perplexing enough to the average man. The law courts in *Bleak House* and the circumlocution office in *Little Dorrit* should not be forgotten when reading Kafka. More than this, the ordeal by inquisition, by Gestapo, by concentration camp, can break men down in much the way that K. is broken. It is no new thing for an individual to find himself helplessly at the mercy of a vast, and hostile, and morally inexplicable machine.

Even on the political level then (which in *The Trial* is the level on which the literal meaning moves), we must allow that K.'s emotions are in great part accounted for by his situation, and that the situation is one that remains permanently possible for us all. The most important meaning, however, is the allegorical one, and here, unless religious experience is thought to be wholly a subjective illusion, we must again allow the appropriateness of K.'s emotions. At this level, he is Everyman face to face with the enigma of the universe—"Everyman," that is to say, faced with the doubt, perplexity and fear of our times. As Everyman, he is on trial before a tribunal whose very rules and requirements and nature are, to him, of the most inscrutable kind.

To assert this is not to deny that K., and his creator Kafka, belong to a minority temperament, and are perhaps more continuously and even unhealthily preoccupied with religious problems than the generality of mankind. It is, however, to assert that the problems dealt with in *The Trial* are real, and not imaginary, and of the kind which no sensitive man can evade. It is to assert also that Kafka's mood, even though it is a personal and perhaps a specialised one, manages at the same time to be the mood of a whole generation. In expressing psychological truths about himself, he was expressing imaginative truths about the dilemma of modern man. The malaise of K. is not that of one man only; it is a malaise of the spirit and understanding of the twentieth century. This, therefore, is the true "centrality" of *The Trial*; and this is the reason why it will remain an important imaginative document of the human spirit even when the spiritual crisis of the age which produced it has passed.

What, then, is this malaise? Kafka nowhere defines it; but I have come to feel that the key insight is moral and relates, perhaps surprisingly, to the hero's character. Instinctively, no doubt, we are on Joseph K.'s side, through the kind of self-identification prompted by fear. But as soon as we think of him objectively, it is clear that he is a somewhat unpleasant man, selfish and lustful, petty and vain. He responds to his inferiors at every point in the novel with arrogance, aping the court officials whenever he can. There is nothing in him of human generosity or religious vision; he has no natural or supernatural resources against the charge of "guilt." In this, his mentality colours events, contributing more to the nightmare than at first we might suspect.

To see this is to notice, among the constructional feature of *The Trial,* the oddity of our relationship with K. In *The Turn of the Screw* we are engulfed in the narrator's vision and allowed "out" only through the most oblique hints. In *Death in Venice* we are close to the hero's consciousness but not contained in it, and free to respond simultaneously as if from within and without. *The Great Gatsby,* on the other hand, presents its hero through a narrator who is in the first place hostile to him and later partially on his side, but each time for reasons strongly personal to himself. *The Trial* might seem closer in this aspect to James than to Mann or Fitzgerald, but the total effect is not really like that of James. Though the narration keeps very close indeed to K.'s consciousness, there is a curious—almost Brechtian—alienation effect. Despite our empathy with K., based on fear of his predicament, there is a continuing neutrality of tone. Just at times the narrator's reflections depart from K.; but always they leave the reader considerable freedom to judge. It is true, no doubt, that the freedom is qualified, much as it is in a strong and compulsive dream. But we are aware of moral defects in K. right from the start, and these become part of our awareness of the trial itself. It is not, I have urged, that he seems mad in the manner of James's Governess, but rather as if his mind is a kind of distorting glass. The Governess seems mad partly because, if we escape her vigilance and imagine the real situation, it is to realise that madness explains things more normally, and more entirely, than ghosts. But K.'s situation is too allegorical to be imagined apart from him: it has to be seen rather as the background to his search for "truth." It has to be seen as the mind's probing of a religious predicament: and when it is, a dramatic new perspective appears. May not the most significant aspect be, after all, K.'s refusal of guilt: his willingness to believe almost anything except that the charge against him is true? He is accused of guilt by powers far greater than himself, and traditionally reverenced by all Jewish, Christian and Hellenic minds. In the Old Testament man confronts a holy God in judgement, and knows himself degraded and lost. He calls upon God de profundis, loving the Law, but broken under its yoke:

I am counted as one of them that go down into the pit: and I have been even as a man that hath no strength.

Free among the dead, like unto them that are wounded, and lie in the grave: who are out of remembrance, and are cut away from thy hand.

Thou hast laid me in the lowest pit: in a place of darkness, and in the deep.

Thine indignation lieth hard upon me: and thou hast vexed me with all thy storms.

Thou hast put away mine acquaintance far from me: and made me to be abhorred of them.

I am so fast in prison: that I cannot get forth.

My sight faileth for very trouble: Lord, I have called daily upon thee, I have stretched forth my hands unto thee.

Dost thou shew wonders among the dead: or shall the dead rise up again, and praise thee?

Shall thy loving-kindness be shewed in the grave: or thy faithfulness in destruction?

Shall thy wondrous works be known in the dark: and thy righteousness in the land where all things are forgotten?

(Psalm 88:3–12; Coverdale translation)

This consciousness is not peculiar to the Talmud (which certainly influenced Kafka), but pervades every part of the Jewish revelation. And we find it also in Plato, and in St Paul—this sense that man moves in the world as an alienated being, cut off from his true life, yet as much the agent of his catastrophe as its victim. The New Testament calls upon men to know themselves under the aspects of Sin, of Righteousness and of Judgement; and this knowledge has always been the path by which European man has reasserted his dignity, saved his sanity, when tempted to deny beauty, holiness, God from the depth of despair. It is the man who knows himself vile and accepts guilt who is able to live again.

The Three Endings of Josef K.
and the Role of Art in *The Trial*

Walter H. Sokel

As with the tip of an iceberg, the visible part of *The Trial* is borne by a submerged part of repressed alternate possibilities in which Kafka's real intentions concerning K. are revealed with relative clarity. This is especially true of the two alternative endings of Josef K.'s life, resp. his trial, which K. dreams. Neither dream was admitted into the novel. One was published separately, in *A Country Doctor* volume under the title "A Dream"; the other, which concluded the chapter "The House," was crossed out by Kafka and suppressed altogether. Comparisons of these dream endings with Josef K.'s end in the novel will make *The Trial* appear as something like the negative of K.'s dreams. The nature of these dreams as well as the fact of their excision shed an important light not only on the truncated text of the novel itself, a fragment despite its ending, but on Kafka's total oeuvre as it presented itself at this exact midpoint in his career as a writer.

The parallels between Josef K.'s execution in *The Trial* and his death in "A Dream" are very strong. In both cases an inner "duty" seems to compel K. to his death. In K.'s waking life, it is the Court, through its executioners, that brings this "inner law" to K.'s consciousness; in his dream, it is an artist. In the novel, he realizes "that it would have been his duty to seize the knife, as it traveled from hand to hand above him, and plunge it into himself." In "A Dream," two men, who correspond to the two executioners in the novel, hold

From *The Kafka Debate: New Perspectives for Our Time*, edited by Angel Flores. © 1977 by Angel Flores. Gordian Press, 1977.

a gravestone in the air and as soon as K. appears, thrust it into the ground so perfectly that it stands "as if cemented there." But from behind the executioners a third man emerges "whom K. immediately recognized as an artist." At once the artist sets to work inscribing on the gravestone with "golden letters" issuing "from an ordinary pencil . . . HERE LIES." But something impedes him; he cannot continue his work; "he let the pencil sink and . . . turned towards K." K. feels miserable. The artist's frustration grieves him; he cries and sobs into his hands. The artist tries to go on with his work, but the former luster of the golden letters fades and is gone. With great effort, he manages to write a capital J—Josef K.'s first initial—but then loses his patience and stamps on the grave mound. "At long last K. understood him." With his bare hands, he rapidly digs his own grave and sinks into it. While K. is "received by the impenetrable depths, his name on high was racing with mighty flourishes across the stone. . . . Enchanted by this view, he woke up."

In K.'s dream the artist assumes the role of the Court in making K. aware of his destiny. In both death is seen as a duty, a personal law which both times K. seeks to obey. In both works, K. while alive is felt to be an obstacle to someone else's progress. In "A Dream" this is transparent. In *The Trial* it is expressed with extreme indirection and subtlety. When on his second Sunday in the Court, K. forays into the attic where the offices of the Court are located, he feels sickened by the close air. "The girl" who is a member of the Court bureaucracy points out to him that he cannot stay because he would "disturb the intercourse (or traffic)" and "K. asked with his glances what intercourse (or traffic)" he was disturbing. The German word used by Kafka in this passage is "Verkehr" which can mean both "traffic" and "intercourse," and thus includes not only the spatial and commercial, but also the sexual aspect of interaction among human beings. We find here an obvious echo of the concluding words of "The Judgment"—the "unending *Verkehr*" which coincides with and outlasts Georg Bendemann's self-removal from life. His death brings back infinite life to the bridge that had seemed lifeless when he had been alive. We are likewise reminded of Gregor Samsa's self-removal from his family which, as the last scene of the story makes abundantly clear, is only now enabled to reenter that stream of procreative life which Gregor's existence had seemed to dam up and inhibit. The "severely" beautiful girl of the Court is coupled with a male figure, the Court usher who had let K. into the Court offices. The pair confronts him, "looking at him" in such a way "as if in the next minute some great metamorphosis would have to happen to him which they did not want to miss." The standard English translation uses the word "transformation," instead of "metamorphosis" for the German word "Verwandlung" which has both meanings. Thereby it obscures Kafka's important verbal reference to his earlier work "Die Verwandlung" (The Metamorphosis) which only consistent employment of the same English equivalent for Kafka's term is able to convey. In addition to the allusion in the term "metamorphosis," a subtle connection between Gregor Samsa's fate and the Court offices of *The Trial* is established.

In *The Trial,* that totally excluding and absolutely alienating phenomenon, the metamorphosis, remains a metaphor even as K.'s inhuman degradation at the end is restricted to the simile "like a dog." Yet, from the vantage point of the last chapter, the banishment from the human race implied by the narrator's use of the term "metamorphosis," even though restricted to the metaphoric, sheds light on the important parallelism of structure between the novella of 1912 and the novel of 1914. In *The Metamorphosis,* Grete makes Gregor understand that he has no place among the living and that had he been human, he would have vanished long before of his own free will. In the last chapter of *The Trial,* Fräulein Bürstner, or a woman resembling her, convinces K. of "the worthlessness of his resistance" to his executioners. From then on he himself leads the way to his death. In both works, the female figure, articulate or symbolic voice of the power system that, at the same time, represents life itself, enlightens the protagonist about his fate. She teaches him that for him self-destruction is the only self-fulfillment.

In K.'s dream, his existence also forms an obstacle, but not to "intercourse." His life blocks the progress and fulfillment of the artist's work. The artist in "A Dream" performs the work of "the hammer" which, Kafka felt, had "to smash [him] to bits" before the onrushing flood of his visions could be "liberated." The threefold division of labor in "A Dream"—between the artist, K., and K.'s name—reflects the structural relationships within Kafka's masochistic and sacrificial poetics. The artist corresponds to the murderous demand of literature for the sacrifice of life. K. corresponds to the living self that is to be sacrificed to literature. The glorious characters of K.'s name on his grave symbolize the visionary work of Kafka's "dream-like inner life." In the period between *The Metamorphosis,* and *The Trial,* the beneficiary of Kafka's scapegoat figure changed from the family to literature. For the "liberation" of his "dream-like inner life," Kafka had, shortly before he began *The Trial,* renounced his engagement. His empirical life was to be a sacrifice on the altar of his work. Even in the midst of his courtship of Felice, more than a year before he began *The Trial,* Kafka had indicated the necessity of this self-immolation. In a diary entry of June 21, 1913, he writes: "This monstrous world which I have in my head. But how to liberate myself and how to free it without being torn apart. And yet [it is] a thousand times better to be torn apart than to keep it locked or buried in myself. For that purpose I live on earth; that is utterly clear to me." Like the penal apparatus of "In the Penal Colony," the artist of "A Dream" embodies the mission of "literature" as a fatal duty and at the same time as a redemption that raises the self to a bliss greater than any happiness ordinary life can offer. Both apparatus and artists are "writers," one writing the sentence of punishment into the prisoner's flesh, the other immortalizing K.'s name high above the body that sinks into oblivion.

This diary entry of December 26, 1914, close in time to the actual composition of "A Dream," stands in an even closer thematic relationship to Kafka's visionary short tale. His redemption, Kafka says here, will come not by literature, but by death. "Do I complain in these pages [of his diary] in order to find redemption in them? From this notebook it [redemption] will not issue; it will come when I am in bed and it will turn me on my back so that I shall be lying beautiful and light and bluish-white; no other redemption will ever come." Comparing this remarkable diary entry with the description of K.'s dying in "A Dream," one is struck by the almost identical wording of the passages. K. sinks into his grave "turned onto his back by a gentle current." The beauty, lightness, and bluish-white appearance, with which Kafka visualizes his own corpse, conveys an analogous feeling of supreme contentment, and indeed delivery, as that which animates K.'s dreamed death. Both death scenes are related to and take the place of literature.

Dying is seen by Kafka as the parallel road to writing, but one that leads further and more effectively to the common goal—redemption. Seen in this context, the artist is not only the embodiment of the writing self that kills and sacrifices the living self for the sake of literature, but he also continues the line of Kafka's Oedipal father

figures who, from Old Bendemann to the two old executioners of
The Trial, cause or demand the protagonists's death as the fulfillment
of a "special law." Impatiently stamping the grave mound, and chasing K. down into his grave, he particularly resembles the archetypal
Mr. Samsa, stamping, hissing, and chasing his son into his room
which is to become his grave. The artist too shows that the protagonist's "duty" lies in erasing himself from the living. At the same
time, however, this artist-executioner of "the dream" reveals the
remarkable transformation which Kafka's Oedipal power figure undergoes in the period of *The Trial* and "In the Penal Colony." For
K., as for the Officer of "In the Penal Colony," death ceases to be a
punishment or even a sacrifice and becomes a treasured end in itself.
With this the Oedipal father figure changes from the protagonist's
master to his instrument. He frankly serves the latter's experience of
delivery.

The close parallel between K.'s dream and the Officer's yearning in "The Penal Colony" is immediately apparent. K.'s "enchant-
ment" is the experience of "being written" even as the Officer's
coveted goal is the experience, and not the discovery, of the "sentence" that is to be engraved in his flesh. However, "A Dream" goes
beyond "The Penal Colony" in making the punitive agency subser-
vient to the self. Although the Officer's goal is utilization of punishment as the instrumentality for pleasure, the content of his
experience is still to be the reception of the "law" into his flesh.
Although this law in his case is self-given and self-administered, it
still is separate from his self. The Officer searches for the aggrandizement of self by the experience of something distinct from and
higher than the self, by the experience of "a law" that forms part of
a power structure or penal system external to the self, a creation of
the quasi-divine father figure of the Old Commander. Josef K.,
however, experiences no "law," no "sentence," other than the glory
of his name. His ecstasy derives from knowing himself abstracted
into his pure sign, his essence, his name. By virtue of this distillation
he is allowed to shine with a splendor that his mere empirical self
could never hope to attain. The transformation of life into literature,
i.e., the change of the living self into its sign, gives such joy that
death is more of a prize to be seized rather than a price to be paid.

Josef K. in the novel is closely linked to Josef K. in the dream.
It is for his name, his good repute, that K. consents to die at the end
of *The Trial.* The admonition which Fräulein Bürstner's shape con

veys to him is partly the condemnation of his will to live, of his ardent possessiveness with which as if "with twenty hands" he had wanted "to snatch at the world . . . and not for a very laudable motive either." But his wish to leave a good name behind seems to be even more important to K. "Am I to show now that not even a year's trial has been able to teach me anything? Am I to exit as a slow learner? Should they be able to say of me after I am gone that at the beginning of my trial I wanted to finish it and at its end to start it all over again? I don't want people to be able to say that of me afterwards." Thus K.'s acquiescence to his execution is only for the smaller part an acceptance of guilt and atonement. For the greater part it is self-regard for the survival of his image. This is a version—greatly subdued to be sure—of those intimations of immortality which the "gilded" letters of his name evoke in K.'s dream. In both cases the self is to be freed from the sullying admixtures and demeaning ambiguities of life. It is to be perpetuated in its desired essence, as a purified image or beautified form—we remember the "mighty flourishes" which K.'s name has become—for others to remember and to behold.

Although explicitly stated only in the last chapter, implicitly this tendency is inherent in K.'s whole struggle for the Court's recognition of his "innocence," and it thus supplies the key to the subliminal drift of the work. In Josef K.'s behavior toward his trial, two basic tendencies are discernible once his initial pretense of disregarding and belittling it is seen through. One is to provoke the Court into punishing and destroying him; the other is to force the Court to recognize him at his own evaluation, as "guiltless." In the later chapters of *The Trial,* K. holds on tenaciously to his claim for a supreme prize—real and definitive acquittal. It makes him ignore and, tacitly or overtly, reject the possibilities for survival by procrastination which Huld and Titorelli seem to offer to him. Against their counsel, K. holds out for an existence justified and confirmed by the highest authority in his ken.

K.'s behavior in his trial parallels the rushing motion and overpowering "pull" which in his dream carry him swiftly toward his grave. In his dream, K. "glided along" on the paths of the cemetery, "as if on a rushing stream," and when he arrives at the grave mound, "the path went rushing on under his shifting foot" so that "he tottered and fell on his knees just in front of the grave mound." This rushing movement toward an imminent and abrupt ending also characterizes K.'s actions in his trial. K. rushes toward a verdict. From its very inception, he seeks a quick end of his trial. Even at his arrest, he obliges the demands of the warders for a black jacket because he is determined to do anything that might "accelerate the matter." He heeds the telephone summons of the Court in order to put an end to his trial once and for all. "This first interrogation must also be the last." Later he is dissatisfied with Huld because of the lawyer's slow interminable pace, and decides to dismiss him because he "could not tolerate obstacles in his trial which were perhaps caused by his own lawyer." He fails to accept, or even consider, Titorelli's counsels because they would either lead, as in Ostensible Acquittal, to a repetition of the trial, or to its indefinite procrastination, in Titorelli's other course. The lawyer calls K. "impatient" and his counsel exactly parallels Titorelli's. He advises seeking every means to postpone judgment and warns of rushing precipitously toward it. His old client Block is the obvious example for K. to learn the patience and concomitant humility which the ability to wait over protracted periods of time expresses. Titorelli generalizes Huld's advice into systems of dodging definitive judgments, and in contrast to the lawyer, actually gives K. cogent logical arguments why dodging is essential for survival. For any verdict known to experience is a verdict of guilty. Thus both Titorelli and Huld adumbrate the position of the doorkeeper in the parable who withholds permission to enter the law. By rejecting such counsel, K. rejects waiting as a condition of existence and insists on rushing toward his judgment.

Georg Bendemann in "The Judgment" also rushes to carry out the judgment against him. In contrast to "The Judgment," however, the verdict is never pronounced in *The Trial*. It is merely executed. The only voice coming anywhere near articulating a judgment, in the sense of supplying a reason for execution, is K.'s own. From the very beginning of his arrest, K.'s inner tendency is to arrive at a verdict which no one gives him and which he finally gives himself.

There is a third ending of K.'s trial which Kafka later discarded, but which also exerts a powerful subliminal influence upon the novel. In the fragmentary chapter, "The House," K. muses on the possibility of persuading Titorelli to lead him to "the office . . . from where the first denunciation in his case had been issued." Reaching the house, K. undergoes a glorious "metamorphosis"; the word "Verwandlung" strikingly refers to Kafka's earlier tale of punishment and sacrifice. But this "metamorphosis" is the complete op posite of Gregor Samsa's. It is a miraculous elevation from "the low life he had led until then" into a radiant, ecstatic condition. "The light that had until now come in from behind, changed and suddenly streamed in dazzlingly from the front. K. looked up, Titorelli nodded at him and turned him around. . . . K. was wearing a new long and dark garment, it was pleasantly warm and heavy. (He) knew what had happened to him, but he was so happy that he did not yet want to admit it to himself. In the corner of a corridor, on one wall of which great windows were opened, he found his former clothes in a pile."

This turning around of K., the 180° shift of the source of light, and the change of K.'s garments—all translate into event the metaphors contained in such concepts as "transfiguration" (in which "metamorphosis" receives a solely positive meaning), "regeneration," "rebirth." The idea of "rebirth" enacted in these happenings of K.'s reverie clearly links "The House" to the fragmentary "Mother" chapter. In both, K. thinks of returning to an origin—in the "Mother" chapter to the origin of his life, in the "House" chapter to the origin of his trial. But in the "Mother" chapter, K. realizes that any hope for delivery placed in this return must be futile; in "The House" reverie, on the other hand, return brings salvation. Unlike Georg Bendemann, Josef K. does not reach a merely symbolic reconciliation with his accuser and judge, but a literal one. He does not atone, he is redeemed.

It is not difficult to see in K.'s reverie a transparent aspect of Kafka's personal myth, the eternal dream of reconciliation with and justification by the parental power to which he owed his life together with his life-long sense of guilt. But here this dream merges with its opposite, Raban's dream of narcissistic omnipotence through total withdrawal from all "engagement" in human life. The artist, Titorelli, becomes the doorkeeper who, in contrast to the doorkeeper in the priest's parable, does lead into the law which is the place, the *locus amoenus,* where justification and liberation are one. The artist is the guide for K.'s return trip to his accuser. In K.'s waking life, Titorelli tells him the only cases of real acquittal are reported in ancient legends. Thus acquittal appears as a return to a remote and nonremembered past, a past of myth and legend rather than of recorded memory. In waking life, not even Titorelli is able to offer an approach to that redeeming past which seems such a close parallel, indeed a variant, of the entrance into the law. But in reverie and dream the artist can be used to effect it. Titorelli's dream service goes even beyond the artist's in "A Dream." In "A Dream" K. has to pay for his transfiguration with his life. Titorelli, however, demands no price at all for the transfiguration procured by him for K.

Titorelli, we remember, turns K. around and the light that had hitherto been behind now shines at him in front. So blatantly does Kafka show that K.'s trial is the negative of K.'s dream of redemption. What looks negative to K.'s waking mind—arrest, accusation, judgment, punishment, Court—is turned around in his dreams and transformed into the instrument of bliss.

Even by such an apparently minor feature as the use of the image of water does Kafka point to that reversal of evaluation. In K.'s waking life, which is his trial, only the negative side of the image of water—with its roots in an early childhood memory is allowed to appear. In the third chapter of *The Trial,* K.'s condition in the Court offices is compared to "seasickness," the same malady which in "Description of a Struggle" conveys the disorientation of the protagonists in the face of the utter incapacity of words to cope with the objects they are supposed to designate. The incommensurability between human consciousness, as organized in language, and the being of things outside this consciousness is repeated in the utter incompatibility between K.'s breathing and the air of the Court. Not until he gets outside the Court offices, can he breathe freely and normally and "at once regain all his forces," while now conversely the Court employees, "accustomed as they were to the air of the bureaus, felt ill in the relatively fresh air" coming in through the open door. Still inside the Court offices, K. "felt he was on a ship rolling in heavy seas." With the same metaphor seasickness or nausea—the etymological root of nausea is "ship sickness" (*malum navis*)—Sartre more than twenty years after *The Trial* described man's unsettling exposure to the existence of things which is forever alien and impervious to human consciousness. In Kafka, as in Sartre, seasickness ("nausea") conveys the bewilderment, helplessness, and terror of the human self suddenly confronted with a world that utterly transcends any hope for comprehensibility, familiarity, and protection. We remember from another of Kafka's early works, "The Stoker," that it is the sea, the liquid element in its largest extent, that gives rise to that profound anxiety which K.'s seasickness like the Fat Man's and the Praying Man's of his earliest work expresses. "A movement without end, a restlessness transmitted from the restless elements to helpless human beings and their works!" And like Georg Bendemann, Josef K. looks down upon a river on his way to his execution.

But in K.'s dream the function of water is reversed. A powerful current sweeps K. toward fulfillment, washing away all obstacles and freeing him from gravity. When Titorelli leads him to the dream Court, their effortless rise and descent on the stairs is compared to the "easy" course of "a light boat in water." And in "A Dream," as we have already seen, the simile of "rushing water" describes the rapid movement of the pathways which carry K. toward his predestined grave, and as he sinks down into the depths of the earth, it is again a "current,"—"gentle" this time—that turns him on his back so that he can look up as "his name up there swept with mighty flourishes across the stone." The image of current or flow has evolved from the fearsome threatening force of an avenging and menacing power into the vehicle of the self's aggrandizement and transfiguration. In his waking state, Josef K. still experiences the Court, and with it the image of water, in its earlier threatening guise; but in his dream, authority cannot resist the flow of inspiration in which all obstacles are overcome. In both dreams the artist is the conveyor to transfiguration. Titorelli transforms the Court, at K.'s behest, from an accusing to a redeeming authority. In K.'s reverie, Kafka portrayed Titorelli as the artist who could lead the self back to that accusatory father figure from whom both guilt and existence issued. Art might effectuate the plea which would transform the accusation into acceptance. K.'s reverie of Titorelli represents a utopian contrast to Kafka's own view of his writing expressed in the "Letter to His Father." There he describes it as a "purposefully drawn-out farewell." But through the dream figure of Titorelli, art brings about not departure, but arrival.

Even though K. excised this dream from *The Trial,* its undertow can be detected in K.'s insistence on "real and definite acquittal." In the guise of the Court's affirmation of his innocence, K. looks for redemption. The headlong rushing toward his verdict, typical of the time structure of K.'s behavior in the trial, receives its full meaning only from the excised dreams.

But the fact of their excision is perhaps even more important for understanding Kafka's full intent in *The Trial.* In this respect, the figure of the painter Titorelli plays a crucial role. In Titorelli's contradictory attitudes, Kafka presents the contrast between art as dream, wish fulfillment, and vision, and art as demythologizing self-preservation.

In K.'s actual encounter with the painter, in the seventh chapter of *The Trial,* Titorelli warns him that real acquittals occur in legends only and are unknown to experience. That is, existence appears justified only in myth. Proofs of real acquittals do not exist, even as the proofs of revealed religion are contained only in documents which the secularist mind declares to be myth. Sensory experience cannot verify them. Titorelli consigns the reports of real acquittals either to faith or to art. He calls them "beautiful," a fine subject matter for paintings. Nor should they be ignored; "they probably do contain a certain truth." But the only place in which this "truth" manifests itself is myth. That is, the ancient legends of real acquittal represent the refuge of a possible symbolic significance. Like a "realist," Titorelli establishes or accepts a cynical dichotomy between what should be and what is, between the "law" as idea and empirical reality. Experience and the law are "two different things" which should not be "confused." "In the law . . . we are told of course that the innocent is acquitted, but, on the other hand, we are likewise told there that judges cannot be influenced. But from my experience I have learned exactly the reverse. I don't know of any real acquittal, but of many cases of pull." He who wants to survive must not permit the theoretical hope for acquittal, the ideal portrayed by art and legend, in other words, "the law," to mislead him. Guided only by empirical experience he must lower his sights, stick to observation, and renounce the expectation of final answers. He should not overestimate the judges. In fact, he should hold them in low esteem, realize their weaknesses, vanities, venalities, and play on their unlawful but all too human character. Above all, he must make the supreme sacrifice and renounce all desire for the unknown and unknowable Highest Court, which alone can grant real acquittal. The Highest Court "is totally inaccessible for you, for me and for all of us. What things look like there, we don't know and incidentally, don't want to know." As there is no salvation and no justification for human existence, without God, neither is there real acquittal without the Highest Court. However, it is only the renunciation of this hope which permits the trial to stay within the limits that make survival in it possible by virtue of the indefinite postponement of a verdict of guilty, which is the only kind of verdict known.

Here the difference between Titorelli's advice and the hope by which Block and the man from the country are reduced to canine existence should be pointed out. Block and the man from the country allow themselves to be degraded because they never cease to hope for acquittal, resp. for the entrance into the law. This hope they share with K., even though they are willing to wait for its fulfillment indefinitely, while he is not. But Titorelli counsels the abandonment of all hope for anyone relying on experience. Only by absolutely believing in his innocence, contrary to all evidence gathered from experience, could K. hope for real acquittal. As I have pointed out elsewhere, Titorelli's radical equation of innocence with faith contrary to reason makes his advice identical with the meaning of the priest's parable "Before the Law," in which the only possibility for the man's entrance is the enormous risk of walking through the gate despite the prohibition by the doorkeeper and his horrifying information about the interior of the law. Titorelli's counsel, however, differs from the priest's "legend" by its point of emphasis. The legend emphasizes the risk attendant upon faith, while Titorelli stresses keeping out of the law in order to survive. He thus anticipates the point of view of the ape in Kafka's parable "A Report to an Academy." The price that the ape has to pay for a relatively acceptable "way out" of the disaster that has overtaken him is the renunciation of all hope for true freedom. As the ape by his renunciation helps himself out of his cage, Titorelli offers Josef K. a "way out" (in two versions) of the invisible cage of his "arrest" and trial. As in the case of the ape, Titorelli also shows that true freedom, i.e., real acquittal, lies buried in legends of a past as inaccessible to the accused as is the native jungle to the ape. In contrast to these spokesmen of Kafka's middle period—1914–17—the heroes of the family tales of 1912, Georg Bendemann, Karl Rossmann, and Gregor Samsa never yielded the hope for an actual return to or a symbolic reconciliation with, the source of their misfortune and existence.

Titorelli shows the so-called "truth" of myth and art to be useless for survival. If survival is to be the central concern, Titorelli presents a picture of human existence which corresponds in essentials to the world view of the modern secularist, as an examination of the time structure built into his proposed "ways out" will show. The time structure of Ostensible Acquittal corresponds to the scientific view of "truth" as verifiable hypothesis. Ostensible Acquittal is distinct from real acquittal by its totally provisional nature. After he has been ostensibly acquitted, the accused must live in constant expectation of a new arrest. He must be extremely wary and utilize whatever changes might take place among the judges. His "efforts for his second acquittal must be adjusted to altered circumstances and generally be as vigorous as those before the first acquittal." A complete lack of ultimate certainty, security, and freedom characterizes life under Ostensible Acquittal. No state of final harmony can ever be hoped for. Since no acquittal is definitive, the cycle of re-arrests and ever-renewed efforts for new acquittals must go on ad infinitum. It can end only arbitrarily with exhaustion or natural death. Life under Ostensible Acquittal reflects the worldview of modern scientific secularism which knows no ultimate finality and certainty, no definitive answers, no ultimate solutions, no permanent goal, and above all no justification of human existence, and whose sole Absolute is survival. It accepts the alternation of unpredictable contingency—the ever-possible arbitrariness of new arrest—and predictable repetition—ever-new trials with ever-repeated ostensible acquittals. This alternation requires of the accused an ever-ready alertness, patience, infinite flexibility, and preparedness for the utilization of sudden possibilities. It also resembles that "Eternal Return" in which Nietzsche saw the cause of the spiritual nausea of modern man and at the same time, the greatest challenge to strong stomachs and vigorous spirits.

The second avenue for survival, Indefinite Postponement, keeps the trial going at its initial stage, and seeks to prevent its ever coming to a termination. For any termination would seem to be condemnation. The accused and his helper must bend all their efforts toward assuring the permanent procrastination of the trial. The trial has to stay confined to its lowest stages. The means are constant observation of the lowest judges and never-tiring attempts to humor and influence them. The accused must never "lose the trial out of sight." Indefinite Postponement functions analogously to the man's waiting before the door. The lowest judges take the doorkeeper's place. They have to be cajoled, flattered, and influenced, but for a reason exactly opposite to the one which moves the man from the country to bribe his doorkeeper. The judges are to be made to prevent, not to facilitate, the entrance into the law. The method consists in trivializing the trial, in substituting the semblance of a trial for its reality, "turning the trial around and around in the tiny circle to which it has been artificially contracted. . . . everything [is] only apparent, the interrogations, for instance, are quite brief, if one has no time or inclination to go for once he is permitted to excuse himself. . . . it is mainly a matter of reporting to one's judge from time to time just to remind him that one is an accused." One goes through the motions of a trial, but these motions are meaningless. They are not to achieve results, except the single one of not coming to any fruition. Meaninglessness is their sole meaning. Indefinite Postponement reads like a parable of modern religion as exemplified by the Judaism of Kafka's father, religion reduced to a social ritual serving the maintenance of one's standing in the community. Postponement likewise postulates the absence of a teleological development; it refuses to view existence as history.

The difference between the two approaches to survival is only one of emphasis. In Ostensible Acquittal, it lies on effort and concentration; in Postponement the stress lies on observation and on mollifying the power that has arrested and continuously threatens one. Both are alike in shutting out any assumption of a final word in one's trial and thus a meaning in one's life beyond survival. Both courses are the exact denial of what Titorelli can accomplish in K.'s excised dream.

The fact that Titorelli is an artist is of greatest significance. In him, and through him, Kafka presents two diametrically opposed views of art which he later juxtaposes more clearly and definitively in the two artist stories of "A Report to an Academy" and "A Hunger Artist." One is the mimetic or realistic, the other the inspirational and redemptive view of art. In the former the artist counsels the self's survival through the faculties of observation, concentrated effort, and deliberate resistance to the "pull" of self-destructive yearning for an empirically impossible redemption. In the other, the artist speaks of the "beauty" of transcending the fetters of empirical experience, or in Kafka's words, of assaulting "the last frontier of earthly life." The existential poetics which Kafka built into his fiction is more clearly apparent in his subsequent *A Country Doctor* and *A Hunger Artist* volumes. The two aspects of Titorelli, for instance, are beautifully repeated by the juxtaposition of the opening and the closing story of the *Country Doctor* volume. The nostalgia of the lawyer, Bucephalus, who in former times had been Alexander the Great's battle horse, for his master's transcendental heroism finds itself repudiated, at the end of the volume by the ape's resigned exchange of absolute freedom, "freedom in all directions," for a modest "way out" assuring physical survival. The two aspects of Titorelli form an earlier version of this juxtaposition of two contrasting views of existence.

Titorelli says he painted pictures inspired by the beauty of the ancient legends that tell of real acquittals; but he never shows them. What he does show instead, and imposes upon his visitor, are pictures that express the utter monotony of a world from which any hope for change and development has been banished. These are the heathscapes which Titorelli himself admits "are rejected" by "some people . . . because they appear too gloomy." As a startled K. perceives, they are not just similar to each other, they are "the one utterly identical heathscape." Titorelli's actual art then is the precise expression of that artificially maintained monotony which survival through Postponement represents. However, both methods of avoiding an authentic verdict have to do with a certain type of artistic endeavor. As we have noted, both methods are based upon close observation and concentrated effort. They depend upon the correct estimate of observed reality. They thus resemble the view of art as "mimesis," as the reproduction of external reality observed with the physical eye, from which the mental eye, imagination, is not only absent, but with which it would interfere. Thus Titorelli represents two views of the function of art. One is to recapture the beauty of fulfilled hope contained in myth, the other is to show the somber monotony of existence as Indefinite Postponement and eternal recurrence. But K. is allowed only to see the latter. The idealizing task of art is reserved for his dreams which are excised from the novel.

The elimination of K.'s dreams from his story leaves only the gloom to which, according to Titorelli, he is particularly drawn. The ecstatic hope alive in his dreams is absent from the narrative text that describes his fate. Hope is a "negative presence" in the novel. It exists there only by virtue of K.'s rejections of those courses of action that would preclude continuous hope for justification and redemption that inspires his dreams. Kafka is careful to bar the dreams themselves. The exclusion of the dreams has two structural consequences for the novel both of which help explain Kafka's intent in *The Trial*. One effect is to unmask the mythologizing nature of art and to strengthen its demythologizing function. The other is to make K. still more opaque and not to allow him that transparency which his dreams give him.

In *The Trial* art is shown as myth-creating. We see the pictures of judges in Huld's office and in Titorelli's studio and learn about their genesis. In the lawyer's office we see a picture of a judge as a powerful figure about to utter a verdict. Art suggests that meaningfulness that K. himself expects from his trial. The painted judge mirrors his own impatience and craving for judgment. The dynamism that informs his dreams is reflected in the savagely tense dynamic posture which the artist has given to the judge. "The unusual fact [about this picture] was that this judge was not seated there in calm and dignity but . . . as if he were about to spring up the next moment with a violent and perhaps indignant twist in order to say something decisive or even to pronounce the verdict." Art presents the judge in an elevated position and godlike majesty "seated on a high throne," strikingly gilded. At the same time, it debases the accused, "who was to be imagined at the foot of the high stairs" only "the highest of which covered with a yellow carpet could still be glimpsed in the picture." The lowly wretchedness of the defendant, who is not evey worthy to be included in the representation, only heightens the glory and grandeur of the authority figure. On the portrait in Titorelli's studio, the maleness of the judge is emphasized by his beard and bushy brows. He is about to rise threateningly from his throne. In his entourage a female figure of justice, consort and ally of the god-like judge, has wings on her feet which heightens the dynamism of the picture. The judge has the figure of justice painted as the goddess of victory and of the hunt, showing the infallibility of the justice administered by his Court as well as the merciless and violent power with which the Court rules the defendants.

Art heightens the power of the Court by tending to overwhelm and humble the defendant. It serves a ferocious and despotic power. While it may give meaning to the defendant's life, threatening him with a quick terminal point of his trial, this meaning is terrible. It is inimical to human freedom, dignity, and life. As in his description of the penal system of "The Penal Colony," Kafka presents here an aspect of his own art as far as it tends to deify the father figure and thus helps to strengthen arbitrary and irrational authority in general. Günther Anders has seen this tendency as Kafka's primary one. But it would be a misunderstanding of his method to equate such a perspective with the total intent of Kafka's work. For the function of art in assisting the hold of a wrathful authority over the longing hearts of men is precisely what he exposes to our understanding. By having Titorelli explain that the portrait of the judge is not true to life, but on the contrary the obedient execution of the judge's instructions for having himself magnified into a mythic image, which has nothing to do with his real appearance, Kafka unmasks the role of art as the servant of tyranny. Art is shown as the creator of myth in the service of power. The painter does not portray fact, but invents according to the judge's guidelines which aim at giving an elevated, untrue image of him. Together with K., the reader too observes art literally manufacturing myth in its pejorative meaning. Repeating the processes of traditional religious art, Titorelli adds a kind of halo around the judge's head. "K. watched as under the quivering points of the crayons a reddish shadow was beginning to form adjoining the judge's head and passed out beyond its radiating toward the edge of the picture. Gradually this play of shadings surrounded the head like an ornament or a high distinction." Titorelli demonstrates to K. and to the reader an art inventive rather than mimetic, raising reality and transforming it into myth. He shows the appearance of the mythic significance of power as the product of the studio, a fraud serving a petty tyrant's vanity. In and by the very process of being shown as myth-making, art acts as supreme debunker and demythifier. It reveals the semblance of the halo surrounding power figures as artifice, "public relations" and propaganda—basically as plain swindle. Leni in particular teaches K. this lesson. The judge's picture which K. discovers through her, shows a man of imposing height; but as she informs K., in actuality the judge is "almost tiny." He "had himself elongated to a great height on the picture, because he is insanely vain as they all are here."

By putting on the halo, Titorelli is shown as doing two opposite things at one and the same time. He mythologizes and by the very act of visibly mythologizing, he deflates. The novel repeats what the artist shown in it does. It creates the giant Oedipal father figure of the Court, gives it daemonic and quasi-divine appearance, but simultaneously unmasks and deflates what it creates. Neither the mythologizing nor the demythologizing aspect in the writing of the novel provides its exclusive interpretation. As I have tried to show elsewhere, K.'s trial cannot be comprehended by any single interpretation because of the contradictory programs built into it. The fact, for instance, that we gain no knowledge of the Highest Court shrouds it in such an aura of mystery that the idea of the Godhead is inevitably suggested to the reader. However, when we see how the suggestion is literally added by the artist's touches, the novel counteracts its own mythologizing tendency and calls it "bluff." Yet the absence of any explanation of the Court's indubitable power over the minds of men and women counterbalances in turn the demythologizing achieved by showing art at work. Since, however, it is only one mind to whose thoughts we are privy, namely K.'s, the constant alternation between a mythologized and demythologized Court depends on the ambivalence to be found in K.

It is K.'s perceptions and conduct that make the double process of inflating and deflating of the Court come into being for the reader. K. consistently maintains a double perspective on the Court and on authority in general. On the one hand, he sees it in a deflating satirical light. On the other, as he lets his longing for the verdict come to the fore, he mythologizes the Court. In this way, the excised dreams radiate into and suffuse the novel. K.'s wish to enter the Court world, to penetrate it, to be accepted in it is openly voiced by him in "The House" chapter. In implicit form, however, this wish lives in *The Trial* from the beginning. In his very first encounter with the Court, through its warders, K. reveals his desire "somehow to sneak into the warders' thoughts, turning them to his advantage or taking up a residence there." This adumbrates in precise terms his later emphatic thought of joining the Court through Titorelli. "Even then there was a possibility of salvation; all he had to do was to slip into the ranks of those people; even if they had on account of their low position or for other causes not been able to help him, in his trial, they could accept and cover him, indeed they could not refuse to serve him in this way, particularly not Titorelli whose close acquaintance and benefactor he had become." In the third chapter, when K. penetrates the Court offices at the suggestion of the usher, he seems to do so reluctantly and merely, as he says, to prove to himself again how "repugnant" the Court is; but his body rushes up the stairs faster than the usher. While his consciousness resists the Court and pretends lack of interest, his action belies it. His body affirms K.'s desire for the Court which his consciousness does not want to admit. The body adumbrates the dream. In the dream of Titorelli, K. will fly up stairs leading toward the Court; then body and consciousness will be attuned to each other, the self will be one, and therefore transparent.

Kafka makes sure that the contrast between waking life and dream reflects more than K.'s own division between conscious resistance and unadmitted desire for the Court. The narrator insists on employing the demythologizing technique in presenting Court reality. In his dream, K. flies effortlessly up the stairs toward his trans-figuration, but K.'s entrance into the real Court offices looks like the caricature of such wish fulfillment. The narrator shows us that as soon as K. opens the door to the attic, "he would have almost fallen flat on his face because there was one more step behind the door. 'They are not very considerate of the public,' " mumbles K. upon attaining his body's wish for the interior of the Court. In the con-tradictory perspectives of reality and dream, not only K.'s but his creator's ambivalence is clearly seen. However, by excising the dreams Kafka shifted the weights of the scales quite decisively to-ward the demythologizing side. The dreams are the most powerful instances of mythologizing. They show the self's apotheosis through its union with, or its submission to, authority. By taking out the dreams, Kafka leaves in the novel only the negative aspect of this relationship to authority and death, the "shame" without the glory. What the dreams show as positive, actualized, and fulfilled appears in the novel in negative form, as K.'s "no" to a life not owed to the Court.

The Trial is so structured, however, that both dreams, although invisible in the novel, exert a powerful pull on K., which constitutes the greatest peril to his life. This pull is shown in the novel as K.'s proclivity toward self-destruction, on the one hand, and as his tena-cious struggle for a saving verdict, on the other. The intimate inter-play of both these tendencies with each other and with K.'s stubbornly cultivated show of independence and rationality, constitute his be-havior in *The Trial*. Kafka leaves no doubt as to K.'s awareness of the danger which the realm of dreams poses to him. At the beginning of his trial, he tells Frau Grubach that the arrest could never have hap-pened to him in the bank because there he is "prepared"; there he is in possession of "presence of mind." Such things as the arrest can take place only in one's bedroom, soon after waking up, when one is, as K. complains, "so ill-prepared." K. sees survival as the difficult achievement of constant alertness and preparedness against the realm of sleep and dream which, as he mentions in a crossed-out passage, are "conditions entirely different from waking life."

> An infinite presence of mind [*Schlagfertigkeit* which literally means "readiness to strike back"] is needed when one wakes up, so that one can grasp at once everything that had been let go the night before, and make sure that

everything is on the same spot where it had been left. That's why the moment of waking up is the most risky in the whole day; once it is behind you, without your having been carried away from your place, you can be quite confident for the rest of the day.

Here K. himself is aware of that imperative need for concentrated watchfulness and ever-ready observation which Titorelli's schemes of survival demand. Kafka crossed out this passage that would have given K. too great an awareness for a character conceived as self-deceiving and driven. Yet, he left no doubt as to the close connection between K.'s trial and the submerged continent of the self—sleep and dream. The most decisive proof of this is, of course, the placing of the arrest in the protagonist's bed and its coinciding with his waking up from his night's sleep. K. is indeed frequently conscious of his need to be more observant and alert. He is apprehensive about his increasingly frequent lapses of attentiveness and preparedness. He repeats Georg Bendemann's self-admonition "to observe everything exactly," and like his predecessor is incapable of following his own advice. Like Uncle Jacob in *Amerika,* he sees the highly organized life of modern economic man as the ego's most promising defense against the inner and outer forces that threaten individuated existence. In his bank, K. says, he is so much better protected.

> Outside line phone and office phone stand on my desk; clients and clerks come and go all the time, but above all there I am constantly in the firmly coherent context of work and consequently possess presence of mind. There I would actually enjoy confronting such an intrusion.

But any distraction and loosening of attention weakens the defensive organization of the ego, and sleeping and dreaming are of course the worst offenders. As for Gregor Samsa, the couch or sofa (*Kanapee*), seat of day dreaming and distracted flow of thoughts, becomes for Josef K. the locus symptomatic for his increasing defenselessness and deterioration.

In Kafka's universe, self-preservation requires the same single-minded resolve as the entrance into the law. K. says to Frau Grubach that if he had resolutely walked past the warders into her kitchen, "ruthlessly oblivious of anyone stepping into his way," he could have "stifled" the trial in its inception. But K. is as unable to walk out through the door and reach his landlady's kitchen, safety zone of *l'homme moyen sensuel,* as the man from the country is unable to walk in through the door and penetrate the realm of spiritual fulfillment called the law. In Josef K., Kafka presented a figure in whom the will to live as economic man, secularized and self-reliant, is not strong enough to prevail over the twin lures of self-transcendence and justified existence, but too strong to permit what Leni calls "the confession" of these needs.

By his excisions Kafka can be seen deliberately depriving K. and his reader of experiencing that fascination which the movement away from life holds for the author. Thus *The Trial* repeats the central experience of "In the Penal Colony." It withholds confirmation. Pursuing the analogy further, we see Josef K. uniting in himself the functions distributed over Officer and Explorer in "The Penal Colony." K. has to observe in his own dying that meaninglessness of death which horrifies the Explorer in surveying the features of the "murdered" Officer. The excision of K.'s dreams parallels the self-refutation of the ingenious apparatus that, according to the Officer, produces transfiguration through slow capital punishment.

The opaqueness with which the novel ends reflects more than its protagonist's negativity derived from ambivalence. Like the breakdown of the Old Commander's creation, it demythologizes Kafka's myth of redemptive dying. If K. dies in a darkness that is never lifted from his trial, if he dies in a shame that results from total inability to discern any unambiguous reason for action, Kafka prevents the mythologizing element of his art from having the last word. The death of a dog robs not only K., but also the Court of all glamor. The butcher knife, in place of the artist's transfiguring pencil, deflates death as well as the authority that metes it out.

When K. comes to the cathedral, he expects to show an Italian the art treasures of his native city. Instead of the art lover, however, he meets the prison chaplain who, before telling him the legend of the doorkeeper, commands K. to put aside his guide book to the art treasures as "unimportant." In terms of the legend, K.'s dreams show a doorkeeper who leads to fulfillment. This obliging doorkeeper is the artist who works with the "rushing waters" of inspiration. By eliminating the dreams and substituting for them a legend with a most non-obliging doorkeeper, Kafka diminishes not only hope invested in mediators, but also in the inspirational art that two years before had carried him through his composition of "The Judgment" and that had celebrated death and contentment, and finally death and transfiguration. Like its contemporary, "In the Penal Colony," *The Trial* represents a thrust against the myth-making tendency of Kafka's own art. To be sure, he still published "A Dream" and united it with the doorkeeper "legend" in the *Country Doctor* volume. But by entitling it "A Dream," he provided a warning label against mistaking self-fulfillment through dying and death for the representation of any, even a fictional, reality.

The Trial: Structure as Mystery

David I. Grossvogel

The fate of Oedipus hinges on a misreading. The oracle speaks un-
ambiguously but through force of conditioning. Oedipus tries to
read *into* the signs traced out by the gods. The gods know that, one
way or another, Oedipus is fated not to understand. His quick wit
and impetuousness notwithstanding, Oedipus is turned into a plod-
ding and awkward interpreter. His exacerbated attempt upon the
limits of human understanding is reduced, like any other such attempt, to a questioning of the impediment. As in a fluoroscopic
process, what cannot be penetrated contrives the only possible picture of the impenetrable. For Oedipus, the veil that hides the unknown is a *text*.

It is the possibility for his text to be this kind of veil that causes
Borges to turn his text into a *reflecting* surface, a mirror that keeps his
reader out even as it talks to that reader about him and his problematic world. The reader's desire to penetrate the Borgesian surface
makes of him a different kind of reader—a reader conscious of reading. And when the fiction, within whose surface text the reader is
birdlimed (the text as labyrinth, as palimpsest), also speaks about the
efforts of a man (as often as not a reader) to progress beyond metaphysical entrapments, the story makes its appeal to the self-conscious
part of the reader created by the text; the fiction of Borges is then
transubstantiated as it reawakens the reader in a moment of his metaphysical dilemma.

Through an interesting coincidence, the surface of the text hap-

From *Mystery and Its Fictions*. © 1979 by The Johns Hopkins University Press,
Baltimore/London.

pens to be already the special province of a particular sort of critic who is less likely to be engaged by the author's purpose than by the way in which the author went about achieving that purpose. The superficial eye of this kind of critic (like that of a tailor for whom the cowl does not make the monk, or the painter for whom pigment does not turn into a landscape) has the virtue of making its object *real* which, at a greater depth, would be only a semblance: all surfaces, whatever intent is vouchsafed them, have in common this substantiality. When the critic has been encouraged by authors like Borges to look for the substance of the work within its surface, he is the more likely to read the surface of other texts as intention, as Lacan in the case of Poe. But the deciphering of a textual surface that is intentionally indistinct from other phenomenological evidence returns the reader/critic to the existential perplexity of Oedipus. At the ultimate extension of this process, the critic is a psychoanalyst questioning the man (the author) through the utterance of his fiction. When that has happened, the unaffected mystery is located once again, after its avatars as fiction, at its nonfictional source.

A century after Poe, what might have been his private nightmares have become considerably less private. Much of the century's writing assumes that the reader feels less comfortable in a world that seems more alien even as it is better known. When Kafka takes his turn as chronicler, he does not describe the aberration of a single consciousness; rather, he describes the aberration of a world that mocks the obdurate sanity of a single consciousness. The reader recognizes Kafka's strange world in his own familiar malaise, but that very familiarity is strange—it is unable to allay the reader's sense of estrangement. Evolution from the private world of Poe to the public world of Kafka suggests that the specialized probing of the psychoanalyst has become less necessary for an understanding of the author behind his text: Kafka is closer to his reader by virtue of what has happened to that reader since Poe. The affinities between author and private awareness, which the fiction of Poe may well mask for the lay reader, appear on the surface of Kafka's text. Kafka has no story to tell; he conveys a mood, an anxiety—*his* anxiety. He does not comment on the mystery: he and his book are a part of it. In the deceptive hints given him, Oedipus reads a text that alludes to the unknown only through such hints as preserve that unknown. When, for once, the god of the oblique speaks straight, he demonstrates that the impossibility of knowing is in Oedipus: Oedipus, the fumbling reader, is seen fumbling before an obliging text. When Kafka contrives a text that discloses Kafka rather than a fiction, he shows again that the impossibility of knowing is within the one who wants to know. And, like Apollo, he does it for a captive reader. Without the benefit of Borges's mirrors or Poe's psychoanalyst, the reader reads himself in the man writing because even after the veil of Kafka's fiction has been thinned into evanescence, the mystery is still not disclosed—only the author stands revealed as another kind of text to be deciphered within the unending process of reading.

Blanchot, who is not necessarily in disagreement with this "reading" of Kafka, begins nevertheless with a challenge: since the art of writing creates at best a surrogate self, are we not indulging in loose talk when we substitute the man writing for his text? How can I write "I am unhappy," asks Blanchot, without turning misery into *calculation* through the contrivance of a text that *states* my misery? An answer (though not quite the one Blanchot proposes) is that a wholly impersonal contrivance by the author is just as impossible. The least personal statement—the most fictional—is an idiosyncrasy: the voice of the writer is in his words whatever those words say. Blanchot, who concludes that writing can only sham life, also concludes that writing is impossible: the writer's voice, as that voice, cannot sham. And Kafka writes stories whose only subject is Kafka.

The paradox begs the question of Kafka's intent; Kafka is not just an anxious man transcribing an anxiety: no act of transcription is innocent. However much the man Kafka is caught up in his act of transcription, that transcription remains a conscious strategy that is distinct from the intimate sense that impels it. That strategy is affected by the strange persistence of the reader's hope—the reader's desire for his text to have a meaning (that is to say an *end*) that corresponds to his need for his world to have a meaning, to *signify*. The modern reader appears to remain as thralled by his expectation as did previous readers who could assume more legitimately that the book might finally be *closed* and its truth contained, though so much of modern fiction subverts the possibility of closure, resists the possibility of a metaphysical assertion even within the boundaries provided by the physical space of the text.

The success of that strategy can be seen in *The Trial,* a text about the confusion of critics and other readers that adroitly confuses critics and other readers. *The Trial*'s story (before Kafka finally wears out the veil of the story) looks like those of the most fraudulent, and

hence the most comforting, of fictional appropriations of mystery—
the mystery story. Even when his predicament cries out for K. to ask
"why?" he insists on asking, as any ordinary detective might,
"where?" or "who?": condemned by a perverse metaphysics, the
victim argues all aspects of his case except the metaphysical. We
recall from our discussion of Freud [elsewhere] that this refusal to
internalize is necessary for the dissemination of the "unheimliche":
Kafka is conjuring not a metaphysics, but its climate.

That climate results from a world described as a surface (the
resistance to interiorization begins in this kind of description): it is a
staged, artificial, but generally nonsymbolic world; it has the partially comic, partially frightening rigidity of any nonhuman imitation of life. The staged artificiality suggests a self-consciousness, the
felt presence of an observer. "One fine morning," when the day
begins as innocuously as any other for K., he notes among many
familiar reminders "the old lady opposite, who seemed to be peering
at him with a curiosity unusual even for her." K.'s angered exclamation at the presence of the warders confirms their being and their
presence as a dominative intrusion: "It occurred to him at once that
he should not have said this aloud and that by doing so he had in a
way admitted the stranger's right to superintend his actions." The
strangeness of K.'s circumstances results from his attempt to enact
everyday gestures on what is becoming more and more definitely a
stage: "The old woman, who with truly senile inquisitiveness had
moved along the window exactly opposite, in order to go on seeing
all that could be seen." "At the other side of the street he could still
see the old woman, who had now dragged to the window an even
older man, whom she was holding round the waist." "In the window over the way the two old creatures were again stationed, but
they had enlarged their party, for behind them, towering head and
shoulders above them, stood a man."

K.'s sense that the gaze of another is on him represents largely
his altered perception of the world around him; he now subjects
what would be otherwise an unperceived continuation of his existence to the disjunction of analysis so that what should seem natural
appears to be contrived, as when he hears the intimate talk between
Leni and Block: "K. had the feeling that he was listening to a well-
rehearsed dialogue which had been often repeated and would be
often repeated." Only very occasionally does the strangeness of this
staging derive from an actual alteration of K.'s world, as when the

warders first appear in his bedroom, or when, walking along a hall in his bank, K. discovers those same warders being whipped in a closet.

Because the event is staged, it *contains* the actor and limits him. The metaphysical constraint is forever being echoed in the comic reductiveness of functional gestures that have become problematic—as when K. tries to hurry his loud and indiscreet uncle out of the bank: " 'I thought,' said K., taking his uncle's arm to keep him from standing still, 'that you attach even less importance to this business than I do, and now you are taking it so seriously.' 'Joseph!' cried his uncle, trying to get his arm free so as to be able to stand still, only K. would not let him, 'you're quite changed.' " But the implications of this comic constraint extend into the implication of a menace: any attempt at a disengagement from this constraint, however successful the attempt appears to be, leads only to further constraint. Direct confrontation of the impediment may cause it to recede, not to disappear:

> "Here's a fine crowd of spectators!" cried K. in a loud voice to the Inspector, pointing at them with his finger. "Go away," he shouted across. The three of them immediately retreated a few steps, the two ancients actually took cover behind the younger man, who shielded them with his massive body and to judge from the movements of his lips was saying something which, owing to the distance, could not be distinguished. Yet they did not remove themselves altogether, but seemed to be waiting for the chance to return to the window again unobserved.

The futility of even modest gestures to achieve an intended purpose demonstrates through comic reduction the metaphysical verdict of the Court that Titorelli spells out for K.: he is "provisionally free"; definite acquittal is out of the question; only the possibilities of ostensible acquittal and indefinite postponement can sustain the balance of hope and frustration that define the victim once he has begun to question his circumstances.

The comic quality of this artificial world eventually turns into what it was all along—the horror of inhuman motion, a supreme illogicality resulting from the only logic that is possible: somewhat in the manner of Munch's cry frozen within the silence of his canvas, Kafka arrests within the frieze of his denouement K. moving at an ever accelerated pace, and finally at a run, to his own death. What accounts for the comic and the horror is the man at the center, K., not simply an initial but an anthropocentric obduracy, the persistent belief in a world that cannot be subverted "one fine morning" by agents of the unknown; a world in which a sense of boundaries and control makes the question "where?" possible and gives it meaning—along with all other aspects of existence. K. is more than the evidence that Kafka assumes the same expectations in his readers: K. is the encouragement for them to persist, as does K., in those expectations. Kafka's whole strategy of disquietude depends on his ability to counterstate the obdurate normalcy of K. and of a reader who, like K., obdurately requires that normalcy. Kafka thus presents and subverts simultaneously the reassuring surfaces of a familiar world. Henry Sussman notes that this duality reaches the heights of irony in K. himself, whose everyday existence absorbs within its unvarying pattern the magnitude of the abnormalcy that has invaded it: K. goes as far as to abet the conspiracy of which he is a victim whenever he can. K.'s outburst to Frau Grubach (an exclamation later reinterpreted by Groucho Marx) is a comic synopsis of the duality that acknowledges his victimization even as he makes an attempt at self-assertion by assuming the point of view of the victimizers: " 'Respectable!' cried K., through the chink in the door; 'if you want to keep your house respectable you'll have to begin by giving me notice.' "

The power of any self-assertion is ultimately sexual. For K., sex represents, like the rest of his life, the evidence of both a process that continues and its subversion. His desperate need for the familiar, normative world is, in part, libidinal—this is one way of reading K.'s assault on Fräulein Bürstner: " 'I'm just coming,' K. said, rushed out, seized her, and kissed her first on the lips, then all over the face, like some thirsty animal lapping greedily at a spring of long-sought water." His staged world stresses both the reality of closure and the possibility of transcending it, and as a part of him intuits that both the definition and the desire are located within him, he is desperately attracted towards others; communication is a way of transcending, and sex is a way of communicating. But on the unnatural stage, that truth becomes, like all others, constrained and misshapen. When the Court usher's wife leads K. to a part of the Law's library, he discovers obscene books instead of the revelatory texts he had hoped for—and they themselves are emblematically marred, artificialized out of even their erotic meaning:

> He opened the first of them and found an indecent picture. A man and a woman were sitting naked on a sofa, the obscene intention of the draftsman was evident enough, yet his skill was so small that nothing emerged from the picture save the all-too-solid figures of a man and a woman sitting rigidly upright, and because of the bad perspective, apparently finding the utmost difficulty even in turning toward each other.

This stage stunts its actors: when she thrusts herself on K., the usher's wife cannot of course allay the malaise to which her ministrations contribute. She is a part of the circumstances that invert K.'s libidinal assertion: the females around K. turn into hungry, uterine mouths. Montag, Leni, the girls in Titorelli's studio, are sexually aggressive, and the threat of the aggression is magnified by the flawed quality of the pleasure they promise: all have more or less startling physical deformities; Fräulein Bürstner's second incarnation—Fräulein Montag—limps; Leni's two middle fingers are webbed; the girl at Titorelli's who pursues K. most closely is hunch-backed, though "scarcely thirteen years old." The womb that is the promise of selfhood recovered, the ultimate possession of self through possession of another, but that becomes instead a threatening vortex, corresponds to a necessary law of gravity that replaces on this stage the lost possibilities of a motion that might have been willed and effective. The Law is the central evidence of such a process; instead of being a dialectical object contained within the mind, it functions as a kind of monstrous tropism—another form of the vortex: "Our officials," the warder explains, "never go hunting for crime in the populace, but, as the Law decrees, are drawn towards the guilty and must then send out us warders." Its mode describes the sort of process that draws K. into its working from the moment he begins dressing for his part even as he refuses to play his role:

> "What are you thinking of?" [the warders] cried. "Do you imagine you can appear before the Inspector in your shirt? He'll have you well thrashed, and us too." "Let me alone, damn you," cried K., who by now had been forced back to his wardrobe. "If you grab me out of bed, you

can't expect to find me all dressed up in my best suit."
"That can't be helped," said the warders, who as soon as
K. raised his voice always grew quite calm, indeed almost
melancholy, and thus contrived either to confuse him or to
some extent bring him to his senses. "Silly formalities!" he
growled, but immediately lifted a coat from a chair and
held it up for a little while in both hands, as if displaying
it to the warders for their approval. They shook their heads.
"It must be a black coat," they said. Thereupon K. flung
the coat on the floor and said—he did not himself know in
what sense he meant the words—"But this isn't the capital
charge yet." The warders smiled, but stuck to their: "It
must be a black coat."

In the force of this strange gravitational pull, the reader senses
the presence of an alien world—however familiar its surfaces might
be. But Kafka is not satisfied with such reminders. What marks him
as a modern author is his refusal to let the reader find refuge within
that last perimeter of his control—the book. Like Borges or Poe,
Kafka replaces the *idea* of an alien world with the objective *evidence* of
a text. This inhibiting and contrived world is, after all, a real book
that rehearses, within the one who wants to know, the impossibility
of fully knowing. The reader cannot *contain* Kafka's text even though
it presents itself as the form (the mystery story) that most readily
contains mystery.

The evidence of the text is confirmed by the central image: the
Law is a world of books; K. is convinced that if he could read them,
he would win his case—possession of the Word being, perhaps, less
problematic than possession of an other: K. responds to the sexual
blandishments of the Court usher's wife in order to possess the books
that are in the library of the Law (only to find in their stead, as we
have seen, further instances of an unappealing and frustrating sexu-
ality). These books are not, of course, available to K.: those behind
whom the Law hides are the sole repositories of a textual secret. The
Examining Magistrate has, as his only distinguishing prop, a single
notebook:

But the Examining Magistrate did not seem to worry, he
sat quite comfortably in his chair and after a few final
words to the man behind him took up a small notebook,
the only object lying on the table. It was like an ancient

school exercise-book, grown dog-eared from much
thumbing. "Well then," said the Examining Magistrate
turning over the leaves and addressing K. with an air of
authority, "you are a house painter?"

Writing is a lingering activity, even within the deserted Court offices: "Some of the offices were not properly boarded off from the
passage but had an open frontage of wooden rails, reaching, however, to the roof, through which a little light penetrated and through
which one could see a few officials as well, some writing at their
desks." Because he is a part of the Court, Titorelli is the scribe of a
tradition, even though he is a painter. Because he uses a different
language, he *paints* Court legends:

> [W]e have only legendary accounts of ancient cases. These
> legends certainly provide instances of acquittal; actually
> the majority of them are about acquittals, they can be
> believed, but they cannot be proved. All the same, they
> shouldn't be entirely left out of account, they must have an
> element of truth in them, and besides they are very beau-
> tiful. I myself have painted several pictures founded on
> such legends.

What Titorelli's paintings have in common with other texts that
represent the Law is that they cannot be grasped, that they possess
no efficacy, no firm or reliable substance; like the very text given
the reader, the texts of the Law are adequate only to sustain for a
while the hope of the one who inquires of them, not to reward that
hope.

But texts persist in the persistence of the decipherer's hope of
possessing his text: one of the many ways K. is tempted to join the
world of his persecutors is by turning into a writer of his own
script—creating the arcane document that will *stand for him*:

> The thought of his case never left him now. He had often
> considered whether it would not be better to draw up a
> written defense and hand it in to the Court. In this defense
> he would give a short account of his life, and when he
> came to an event of any importance explain for what rea-
> sons he had acted as he did, intimate whether he approved
> or condemned his way of action in retrospect, and adduce
> grounds for the condemnation or approval. The advan-

tages of such a written defense, as compared with the mere
advocacy of a lawyer who himself was not impeccable,
were undoubted.

Writing would represent a new aspect of the same quest for K.: it
would be a way for the patient reader, which the victim—K. or
Block—has already become, to seize his text, instead of being reduced, like Kafka's own reader, to read those reading (writing),
unable as he is to read the text those readers read (or write).

Whatever object the quest may posit, through whatever subter-
fuge, that object remains elusive. The word *God* is absent from
Kafka's fiction, but the Jewish mystical tradition (upon which Borges
also draws) equates for Kafka the impossible revelation and the revelatory letter: it is within scripting signs that the unknowable shows
and conceals itself. The word, as mystical mediator, as initiate, is
caught up in the dialectical process that affects the way in which all
initiates are perceived: it can only state its failure to reveal but in so
doing is suffused with intimations of the mystery it has attempted.
The Kabbalah believes in the occult meaning of the letter, the presence of God in the sign of His word: instead of making God appre-
hensible, this presence makes the letter awesome. We have noted in
our reading of Borges how, in time, this awesome signifier becomes
little more than an amulet, a container suggesting a reversal of the
original denial by offering as *possible* the appropriation of a final and
absolute mystery. But a sacredness attaches to even the ineffectual
amulet (it is for that reason that no amulet is wholly ineffectual).

In Kafka's fiction, the missing term *God* is replaced by His
letter, the Law, an ironically scripted form of the absolute, in the
same way as the letter of this text is informed by the presence of its
own *deus absconditus*—Kafka. "Everyone strives to attain the Law":
K.'s hope, and the reader's, are sustained by an awareness—the importance of the part of themselves that is concealed by the fiction of
their text. For both, the integument of the mystery that cannot be
uttered (as cannot be uttered the name of God) will be the *parable,* the
traditional reduction of that mystery as allegorical fiction.

The parable, a mode in which Kafka showed an abiding interest,
acknowledges intellectual slippage, a failure of the mind to appre-
hend its object. The parable is a *substitute,* a simile. The German
word *Gleichnis* also means simile; its root, *gleich,* evidences the perplexity of knowing: it means both *same* and *resembling*—that is to say,

identical and different. It is not improbable that Kafka favored the parable because he was most intent on demonstrating this slippage, on making the reader experience the impossibility of locating his world anywhere else but in this slippage. In his *Parables and Paradoxes,* he says, "All these parables really set out to say is merely that the incomprehensible is incomprehensible." The parable also contains the tone, the tradition, and the manner of the failure of the hidden god to become manifest. And when the parable comments on the failure of the parable, it merely returns to literature a traditional concealment of god as text.

Long before Kafka turns formally to the parable, he has already constructed a fiction that proves, in the multiple instances of its own slippage, to be more than a mere fiction. And in this endeavor, he is seconded by an ironic fate: none of his major fiction is complete in the form we have of it; in *The Trial,* the very ordering of the chapters is not necessarily Kafka's. It is on this shifting ground that contrives the deceptive revelation of a parable whose magnitude is equal to the totality of the fiction that Kafka establishes a central parable that his fiction treats as a problematic text—a parable whose lesson is the doubtful nature of parables.

Since the parable is a *likeness* that discloses and disguises a more distant truth, what will be the central parable of *The Trial* does not disturb the innocuousness of other events: the self-consciously moral fiction develops within the continuation of an apparently conventional fiction. An influential Italian customer of the bank where K. still works is visiting town and K. is appointed to squire him. Like all other episodic and trivial events within K.'s life, this one contains in germ the mood of, and what might be read as emblems for, something more than the story that those episodes contrive. K's encounter with the Italian visitor in the office of the Manager suggests the inevitable continuation of the perverse law proclaiming that everything that can go wrong will. K.'s knowledge of Italian is tenuous, the Italian speaks fast and lapses frequently into a southern dialect, a bushy moustache conceals the motion of his lips: the problem of understanding signs, of trying to solve the unintelligible, becomes once again a preoccupation of K., within the similar but overriding preoccupations that already perplex him. Once more, K. is outside an event that concerns him but that he cannot penetrate.

The visitor wants to visit the town's Cathedral, where K. agrees to meet him later in the morning. While waiting for that meeting, K.

continues within a life whose normalcy has already become an an-
noying irrelevance. Now, additionally, that normalcy mocks the
urgency of an event: a new puzzlement has thrust itself into a pattern
whose ordinariness has long since been subverted by K.'s other pre-
dicaments. K. is now three times baffled: the routine at the bank
prevents him from refreshing his Italian, which he will need for his
encounter with the incomprehensible visitor; and the visitor, for
whom he must perfect his Italian, provides an additional distraction
from K.'s obsessive need to give all his time to his "case." This tiered
frustration leads him to believe that "they're goading me": as usual,
K. creates an otherness in which to place his dilemma.

K. arrives punctually for his appointment at the Cathedral, but
his visitor is of course not there. Since the central question revolves
around the possibility of *understanding,* K. wonders whether he is in
possession of the correct facts: was the visitor supposed to be there at
all? The day is rainy, the Cathedral dark. A few candles have been lit,
emblematic objects that do not cast sufficient light to see clearly by;
their own true clarity is in their emblematic significance. To their
half-light, K. adds the inadequate light of his own pocket lamp. It
picks out of the gloom the strange figure of a knight in a canvas
against one of the walls. For a moment, the incongruity of the figure
holds K.'s attention. When he moves his light over the rest of the
canvas, it discloses a conventional Sepulture of Christ and he loses
interest. In this rare instance, the normative world dissipates the
question, and K. is no longer able to be held by a normative world.

K. catches sight of a verger who is making signs to him that he
cannot understand: the verger is enacting a role for the benefit of K.
but it is one that K., once again, cannot fathom. The Cathedral is full
of such signs, among them a light over a small side pulpit that is
hardly larger than a niche for a statue. K. is drawn to the pulpit: the
light over it would be "the usual sign that a sermon was going to be
preached." Is a sermon going to be preached there—will there be a
religious discourse delivered for the sake of instruction? The answer
is that a religious discourse will be delivered indeed: the pulpit has
the attributes of height and sanctity from which an absolute truth is
traditionally handed down. But whether instruction will be handed
down as well, or what exactly the form of that instruction will be, is
problematic: instead of the sermon's instruction, Kafka will insert
here the ambiguity of the parable.

In the house of God, and in the accepted manner of any solemn handing-down, a voice calls K. from the pulpit: the ultimate mystery, like lesser ones, states clearly its relation to its object and little more. The voice acquires its resonance not only from the spiritual acoustics of the Cathedral but because it belongs to a young priest who knows K.: he is connected with the Court. Intuiting the ambiguity of what will follow, K. responds only when he has been able to make the unequivocal summons seem ambiguous:

> But if he were to turn round he would be caught, for that would amount to an admission that he had understood it very well, that he was really the person addressed, and that he was ready to obey. Had the priest called his name a second time K. would certainly have gone on, but as everything remained silent, though he stood waiting a long time, he could not help turning his head a little just to see what the priest was doing.

With comic obduracy, and true to his mode, K. tries to reduce the intrusion of a transcendental revelation to the mundane level of his everyday life: "I came here to show an Italian round the Cathedral." So K. must be told what the reader knows already, that this normalcy is "beside the point." The point is that K. is presumed guilty. For one of the few times in his life, K. rebels: if he is guilty, then no man is innocent: "If it comes to that, how can any man be called guilty? We are all simply men here, one as much as the other." The priest acknowledges this similarity but reminds K. that this is nevertheless the talk of guilty men; the condition is not circumstantial and is therefore not subject to rational rejection. The *trial* (in German, *der Prozess*), which is never a trial but simply a *process*, turns into guilt as part of the process: "The verdict is not suddenly arrived at, the proceedings only gradually merge into the verdict." In the *process* of our existence, our *arrest* is nothing more than our awareness, our *trial* the result of that awareness.

This concomitance denies the possibility of melioristic gestures and human contact. The priest is supposed to bring comfort, but however good his intentions, he is likely to harm K. Still, K. is drawn to this figure of good: "With you I can speak openly." The priest's answer is ambiguous: "Don't be deluded"; it may refer to what K. was saying previously, it may refer to what K. has just said. K. attempts to clarify the ambiguity; in response, the priest delivers

Kafka's parable, the similitude that instances an *otherness,* the periphrase whose elaboration confuses.

The parable reinforces within this context notions of mystery, elevation, and final revelation. In a story about the impossibility of passing beyond, the Door (the traditional gateway to a supernatural realm) and the Law loom (like the word of God) before the man from the country. For the reader, the parable also borrows biblical cadences in order to tell about the Door—the uttermost extension of the human possibility, informed with the terrible mystery that it proclaims and protects.

The doorkeeper is the traditional intercessor similarly haloed (though here in a comic mode) by his proximity to the unknown and, in the manner of all intercessors, utterly ineffectual. The door-keeper, like the Door itself, like the priest who tells the story, like the very story of which that story is a part, is on *this side* of the impenetrability: he can only be a distracting focal point. Moreover, he does not keep out the man from the country, and the door is always open; the inability to enter is in the one seeking admission. The priest's critical analyses may be confusing in their catholicity, but they are not necessarily wrong:

> He allows the man to curse loudly in his presence the fate for which he himself is responsible.

> The man from the country is really free, he can go where he likes, it is only the Law that is closed to him, and access to the Law is forbidden him by only one individual.

> There is no lack of agreement that the doorkeeper will not be able to shut the door.

It is the necessary ineffectiveness of the intercessor that allows him even to be kind: "The doorkeeper gives him a stool and lets him sit down at the side of the door"; "The doorkeeper often engages him in brief conversations, asking him about his home and about other matters." The kindness of the doorkeeper, like the consolation of the priest, is of the same order as the impediment that may be forced temporarily to recede, but not to disappear, or the human gesture that achieves an immediate end mocked by the metaphysical dilemma that constrains it.

The man from the country can do only what man has always done before the unknowable: fasten on the figure of the intercessor.

Like Oedipus, like Block, like K. himself, the man becomes a close reader of the surface of an impenetrable text: "In his prolonged study of the doorkeeper he has learned to know even the fleas in his fur collar." As the mystery asserts its impenetrability, man acknowledges his failure to know by deifying the unknown: in an ultimate and self-deriding attempt to contain what cannot be contained, he makes of the mystery God: "In the darkness he can now perceive a radiance that streams inextinguishably from the door of the Law."

But Kafka is concerned, of course, with an entirely different text—there is no man before the Door: there is only a reader, Kafka's, before *his* text. The parable that complicates the complex fiction within which it is set will now be turned into an object lesson— literally, a parafictional object on which the reader will perform the exercise suggested by the fictional characters. The priest, who belongs to the Court, has charitably entertained all of K.'s unanswerable questions; the priest, as critic of the text, will entertain sufficiently numerous and contradictory interpretations to show the impossibility of reading.

The "scripture" related by the priest is both holy and full of holes: it is given as the comfort of a truth recaptured, an absolute that can be comprehended. But modern fiction, perhaps starting with Kafka, opens fiction unto the unknown deliberately, offering itself as experience rather than imitation. The priest is not content to set forth a parable about the impossibility of knowing; he will not lose the reader within the diverse and contradictory possibilities afforded by the genre. Though he is the only speaker of the parable, he cautions K. against hasty interpretations: "Don't take over someone else's opinion without testing it." But there is no "someone else": K. has only the priest's text, just as the reader has only Kafka's; the suggestion is inescapable: though the priest has told "the story in the very words of the scriptures," the very text as text is suspect.

Once doubt has been cast on the body of orthodoxy, its absolute assertion is no longer commensurate with absolute revelation. Any interpretation is possible: "The commentators note in this connection: 'The right perception of any matter and a misunderstanding of the same matter do not wholly exclude each other.' " The scripture therefore invites a gloss that is supposed to provide further steps towards the unknown. But as the gloss is the intercessor of an intercessory text, it represents in fact a step back, a greater distance from the inaccessible truth. Even though K. was admonished by the priest because he had "not enough respect for the written word," that "disrespect" comes from the only posture that is possible before the text: utmost respect; through overly close scrutiny, K. has analyzed the only surface allowed him into meaninglessness. It is through this same kind of gloss-making that the priest now leads Kafka's reader. As the reader is drawn through the maze of the text, he is drawn through another part of his awareness; forced to proceed tentatively through the text, he rehearses the tentative nature of his being, the tentative nature of an existential process of which the book he is reading is now only a part.

For neither K. nor the reader can there be any ultimate revelation. There is only description, necessity: "I don't agree with that point of view," said K., shaking his head, "for if one accepts it, one must accept as true everything the doorkeeper says. But you yourself have sufficiently proved how impossible it is to do that." "No," said the priest, "it is not necessary to accept everything as true, one must only accept it as necessary." "A melancholy conclusion," concludes K., "it turns lying into a universal principle." But such "lying" results only from a confrontation with the absolute; the priest is more philosophical and relativistic—he is, after all, only a part of the shifting boundaries that defeat the possibility of any human grasp.

K.'s light, which the priest gave him to hold, has long since gone out; small loss: it was more limiting than revelatory. Kafka snuffs it out three times: in the cathedral, in the death of K. (our confused eye within this particular text), in the text itself. Like K., and for the duration of the fiction we share, we have been kept at arm's length from something that is important to us and that we can sense only by circling around it. But in our circling we have become K., and we also have been reading about ourselves reading—hopelessly. Starobinski notes a similarity between Dostoevsky and Kafka in that the characters of each no longer have a "chez soi"—they have been expelled from their rightful home, they are in exile from themselves. Kafka's purpose is to make us aware of our own exile, but in the process we have entered his book, we have entered into his sense of the unenterable: *we* now inform the pale surfaces of his story as he first did.

On Kafka's Novels

Martin Walser

THE WRITER—HIS LIFE AND HIS WORK

Franz Kafka is a writer who has assimilated his experience so thoroughly that we have no need of biographical information in order to understand his work. For he has already completed the task of transmuting reality *before* he comes to write his fiction, through the systematic impoverishment—indeed the destruction—of his real-life social self, sacrificed in order that he can create in its place a personality wholly devoted to writing. This literary *persona*—*"poetica personalità,"* in Croce's phrase—determines the form of Kafka's work; so we need to look briefly at the way it evolved.

As Kafka's social self becomes impoverished, so his literary *persona* grows and develops. In his diary he analyses these processes in order to discern the *"pattern* in a life like mine." The relentless impoverishment of his social self becomes necessary because Kafka as a writer is no longer able to cope with life in any other way. But it is precisely this situation which makes writing possible: "The man who can't cope with life while he's living needs one hand free to try and ward off the despair he feels at his own fate . . . but with the other hand he is able to *record* what he sees beneath the ruins; for he sees more things than other people, and different things. He's dead in his own lifetime, you see, and yet he's the one who really survives."

From *The World of Franz Kafka,* edited by J. P. Stern. © 1980 by George Weidenfeld & Nicolson Ltd. This essay was translated by Allan Blunden.

THE MODE OF NARRATION

Kafka writes his stories in the third person and does not appear himself as narrator. (We are referring now to the three novels.) Narration as an aesthetic reality in itself does not form part of the book's actual fabric. Consequently the reader is never addressed directly—an important point, when one considers how freely storytellers throughout history have availed themselves of this device, which remains the peculiar prerogative of narrative writing. (The drama lacks this facility, with the exception of a few experimental works which have tried introducing the author on to the stage.)

[Kafka] is never present as storyteller: the story is simply *told*. He dispenses with this visible narrator, the "creative manipulator," who has even been described as the "*sine qua non* of all narrative literature." What we propose to show is that for Kafka, narration *without* a visible narrator is the *sine qua non,* and that his writing nonetheless remains wholly narrative in character. For him this narrative stance is a necessity, the mode which he found to be best adapted to his own needs. He started writing the early chapters of *The Castle* in the first person, so that to this extent he did "appear" in the novel in the guise of first-person narrator; but later on, in the course of further work on the book, he replaced this first-person form by the use of a third person—namely, K. Thereafter he makes no further attempt to establish a narrative presence in the work.

The light in Kafka's works grows progressively more dim, and his heroes find themselves further and further removed from their goals. These tendencies inevitably serve to diminish the visible solidity of Kafka's narrative world. The hero sees less; therefore he interprets instead. We as readers are totally dependent on this interpretation, since there is no narrator on hand to tell us more than the hero himself sees—for the simple reason that the story is narrated *through* the hero.

Total congruence of author and medium is called for whenever events are leading up to something that is not to be revealed to the hero until later. There are certain developments that begin and end within the individual works, tensions that underlie the action, circumstances that cannot be made known to the hero until after a certain point in time—"revelations," in a certain sense. The atmosphere created by a literary work depends very largely on whether we as readers are made aware of these circumstances right from the beginning, so that we observe the unknowing hero groping his way towards a discovery of them; or whether we ourselves share his ignorance and surprise. If Kafka had wanted to hint at events to come he would have had to distance himself from the hero on occasion, and thereby remove us from the hero's perspective as well.

Here we are concerned with K.'s interpretations of the people and things around him. [These explain] the frequent use of conjectural language. In fact its frequency increases from one work to the next, until in *The Castle* it has become strikingly stereotyped in form. These interpretations, which always point in the same direction, are conveyed without any intervention on the part of the narrator. Their menacing implications for K. are borne in upon us in the same moment that they are perceived by K.—because we only learn of them *through* K. The expressive force of these menacing implications derives not least from Kafka's refusal to step outside the particular point of view from which they are perceived. All is uncertain: "it was not clear whether the contempt in her voice was directed at K. or at her own reply"; "the fact that they knew who K. was did not appear to be a point in his favour." When K. thinks that somebody wants to do him a service, this is his immediate reaction: "His whole manner did not suggest any special desire to be friendly. It was more like a kind of selfish, anxious, almost pedantically insistent attempt to get K. away from the front of the house" [all these quotations are from four pages in the first chapter of *The Castle*].

These interpretations follow a fixed pattern: they are the manifestations of a kind of compulsion always to react in exactly the same way. At the same time the narrative stance adopted by Kafka finds in them its purest form of expression. By telling the story from a single point of view he shows that K. exists in a particular kind of relationship with his environment, and that this relationship never alters. The figure of K. has been intentionally set up—one might almost say "constructed"—in such a way that interpretations of this kind become a recurrent feature of the narrative. So absolute is the congruence of author and hero in Kafka's case that he prefers to turn things upside down and make the hero an enigma to himself rather than consent to intervene with any kind of authorial interpretation. It is just possible that K. himself has thoughts about his own extremist interpretations at some stage—and in fact there is one occasion (but only one) when he admits that he may have gone too far (*The Castle,* chapter 20, in K.'s harangue of Pepi). But then he confirms himself in his original opinion once more and says, "I don't know if that's a true picture of things, but I do know that it's closer to the truth than the picture you paint." Kafka does not intervene himself; he allows the serving girl and K. to present their opposing views and leaves it at that. He simply tries to preserve a balance of interpretation.

But when a narrator appears as a character within the story we are at liberty to "interpret" what he says. This is no less true for Kafka than for any other writer, and we find such an instance in *The Trial,* when the prison chaplain tells the parable "Before the Law." Following on from the telling of this story, Joseph K., together with the priest himself, suggests a number of possible interpretations. But—and this is a point that many Kafka commentators tend to overlook—these interpretations remain contained within the novel: they are not addressed to us, the readers, as a source of reliable information, but are offered for our interpretation just like any other part of the text. It is exactly the same when K. discusses the Castle with Olga; his interpretations, or perceptions of meaning, are open to interpretation in their turn, and carry their own meaning for us, the readers.

A further consequence of the narrative technique practised by Kafka is the irreversibility of the narrative process itself. Nothing can be anticipated, because there is no narrator to signify what is to come. Events simply take their course: nothing can retard the process, nothing can accelerate it, and nothing can interrupt it.

The essential results of Kafka's method [of doing without a "broad" world represented by an independent narrator] are these: the hero's impression becomes increasingly absolute and so, conse-quently, does the reader's; and this in turn is marked by an increased dominance of unsecured interpretations, usually in the subjunctive mode. The work, then, develops from within itself as a process that is irreversible, linear, without commentary, taking place outside any natural time scale.

The world that is narrated in this manner lacks "breadth," in the sense of richness and variety. But the narration itself—and hence the world that it encompasses—is intensive in character. Sartre proposes that we should no longer seek to express "beauty" in terms of "form" or "substance," but in terms of "fullness of being." "We should like our books to float in the air," he writes, "while our words . . . quietly and imperceptibly become sleighs that carry the reader into the midst of a world without witnesses." Such is the situation of Kafka's narrative writing, from which the omniscient narrator—indeed any form of visible narrator—has been finally banished.

FUNCTION AS PERSONAL CHARACTERISTIC: COLLECTIVES

For Joseph K. it is significant that the defendants who fill the interminable attics in the suburb all appear to belong to the "upper classes" (*The Trial,* chap. 3). What is equally significant is that they now constitute, in their capacity as defendants, a new social group-ing, a new class. Like every other class in the structured world of Kafka's fiction, this one has what one might call its characteristic posture: in this case the bent backs and sagging knees that are the result of long periods of waiting in the low-ceilinged attics. As a class they have evolved their own social rules, their own superstitions; they comfort and torment themselves with the formula that waiting is not a waste of time, whereas any form of "independent action" most certainly is. It is essential to keep oneself continually occupied, for there is another rule which states that "a man under suspicion is better off moving than at rest, because the man who is at rest may be sitting in the balance without even realizing it, being weighed along with his sins" (*The Trial,* chap. 8). They even have their social pride: as a defendant Block evidently regards himself as superior to Joseph K. because he crawls up to the lawyer's bed on all fours, while Joseph K. remains quietly sitting down—even though he too is a man on trial.

What these defendants are or were in any other context is of no consequence at all; since the story is told through K., who only sees them as defendants, they possess no other attributes that we know of. They are no longer citizens of the world at large, but functional figures in the artificial world created by Kafka: they have no existence outside their role as defendants. Some are having more luck with their case than others, some submit better petitions than others, and so on; but apart from these minor differences of degree they all appear identical. Kafka has no need of more elaborate characterization; he can achieve his purpose with great economy of means simply by slotting a figure into place within the hierarchy of his structured world. The figure is sufficiently sharply defined by the place he assigns to it. These defendants, viewed as a collective body, have their counterpart in the villagers in *The Castle*. Like the defendants, these villagers only exist essentially in the plural. Just as the defendants abandon themselves unthinkingly to their superstitions and their stereotyped maxims, so "the people [in the village] are busy creating their own confusion" (*The Castle,* chap. 15). "Castle stories" are made up: "there are people here who positively feed on that kind of thing." Like the defendants, they use this kind of talk to comfort and "entertain" each other. K. is conscious that he must become "indistinguishable" from "the peasants" if he is to gain a footing in this situation (*The Castle,* chap. 2). We only ever hear about "the people," "the peasants." They too have their "superstitions," of course (as in *The Castle,* chap. 15) [Amalia's secret], and their own well-defined patterns of gesture and behaviour: their collective pushing and shoving, their habit of always reacting as a group, their timid and sly whispering among themselves, their dull-witted frightened childishness—such are their characteristic ways. K. is able to describe them in a single sentence, compressing their entire existence into a few words: what is more, he can speak of them in the singular, since what is true of one is automatically true of all the rest. He begins with a reference to "their literally tortured faces" and then continues in the singular: "it was as if the skull had been beaten flat on top, and the facial features distorted into their present shape by the pain of being beaten" (*The Castle,* chap. 2). "How humbled they must be," thought Joseph K. when he saw the defendants for the first time (*The Trial,* chap. 3); and exactly the same might have been said of the villagers. Their faceless submission is intended to show K. the power of the Castle: such is the underlying function of this collective body, just as it was the function of the defendants, as a class, to show

Joseph K. what the experience of a trial can do to a so-called human being.

COMPANIONS

The purpose of the figures we shall now consider is to distract the respective heroes to whom they are assigned, making them lose sight of themselves and their objectives.

The "companions" assigned to the hero in *The Trial* are the three junior bank clerks, Rabensteiner, Kullich and Kaminer. It is through them that the world of the Law Court offices, a chaotic world of attics and passageways, makes its entry into the orderly and well-regulated life of the bank. When Joseph K. first finds out about the proceedings against him and is about to return to the bank, these three companions thrust themselves upon him in order to "distract" him (*The Trial*, chap. 1). Through such distraction all the various companion figures seek to make Kafka's heroes lose sight of themselves. The assistants in *The Castle* are given the task of providing K. with "a bit of entertainment" (chap. 16). And distraction is likewise the aim of the two vagabonds in *Amerika*.

It is indicative of the functional character of these companions that Kafka's heroes are not free to choose them for themselves. K. in *The Castle* describes his assistants as "a couple of lads who've wafted down from the Castle" (chap. 18); he has to be expressly informed that they have not "drifted" to his side, but have been "assigned" to him (chap. 5). And just as these assistants have not simply "dropped down from the sky," so Blumfeld's "trainees" have not been assigned to him at random. There is a very definite point to these assignments, and the companions are put there in order to fulfill a distinct function. They come suitably equipped for their task: they are "insignificant, anaemic young men" (*The Trial*, chap. 1) or "silly boys" (*The Castle*, chap. 13), "mere lads, full of high spirits and a little silly" (*The Castle*, chap. 12). One can imagine the kind of tasks to which such companions are suited, just from a brief look at the range of expressive possibilities available to them: Kaminer's "tedious and vacuous liveliness," the way the assistants "hop about" and "fling out their arms" (*The Castle*, chap. 13), while their flesh "sometimes gave the impression that it was not really living," and the way they walk "as though [their limbs were] charged with electricity" (chap. 16), their "whimpering" and tapping on the window panes, their whispering, giggling, sighing, staring, smiling and grinning—such are their characteristic gestures.

If it is true that Kafka's figures acquire their identity through their function, then it follows that they must lose that identity as soon as they step outside their functional role vis-à-vis the hero. In fact the only time this happens is in *The Castle,* when the assistants are dismissed by K. By their dismissal they are made to step outside their function; and with that their whole being—and the way it expresses itself—undergoes a change. The change is almost instantaneous. K. no longer recognizes one of the assistants: "he seemed older, wearier, more wrinkled, but fuller in the face, and his walk too was quite different from the brisk step of the assistants, whose limbs twitched at the joints as though charged with electricity" (chap. 16). In their capacity as assistants Arthur and Jeremias had formed a pair, united by their common mission; but now, after K. has ended their association by dismissing them, their "youthful spirits are quite gone." If the office of companion were to be transferred to someone else, that person would undoubtedly have to adopt the same gestures and modes of expression; for without these he could not fulfill his function as a companion within the general economy of Kafka's structured world.

In *The Trial* too—and even in *Amerika*—there are hints to support our view that Kafka's figures acquire their identity through their function. When Joseph K. summons his three companions at the bank to his office, he finds their manner perfectly normal; they have "become absorbed once more into the general mass of clerks at the bank" (chap. 1). But as he is walking out to the suburbs on the Sunday morning to attend the first interrogation they reappear once more, and now they behave again as they did at the first meeting in Joseph K.'s lodgings: they "cut across in front of K.," "lean inquisitively over the railing" and stare after him (chap. 2); once again they have become disquieting figures who shadow the hero in his movements.

WOMEN

Here too it is clear that Kafka's figures do not undergo any kind of "spiritual transformation." The lives of women [in the novels] contain only superficial change—a change in status, for example, and a corresponding change in the way their presence makes itself felt in the work. Their rank and position within the structured hierarchy of Kafka's world is their one and only important distinguishing characteristic, and one which is reflected in the smallest detail of movement and gesture. This determines K.'s intention toward the "girl from the Castle." She too is to be used in his struggle, since "one must take advantage of anything that offers the slightest hope" (chap. 13). K. does indeed "take advantage" of women, using them as tools for his own ends. We are told nothing about these women unless it has a significance in relation to their function. So, for example, Kafka differentiates hardly at all between the outward appearance of Leni and that of the Court usher's wife: one has "dark, shining eyes" (*The Trial,* chap. 2), the other has "big dark eyes" (chap. 6). But what he does represent in some detail is their functional value, which is measured by the quality of their relations with, for example, the Castle officials.

The landlady of the Brückenhof inn, for instance, is the archetypal ex-mistress of a Castle official (chap. 6). She shows consideration for K. only on Frieda's account. And she does this only because Frieda, like herself, is a former mistress of Klamm's. ("Did I concern myself with you so long as you were on your own?" she asks K., in chap. 4.) Everything we learn about this woman is connected with Klamm: thus she is forced to evict K. from her house "out of respect for Klamm's memory" (chap. 7). The landlady, then, is another figure who has no characteristics of her own; her whole life revolves around Klamm. Although she tells her story from beginning to end, we learn nothing that is not directly related to Klamm. Her function as a figure in *The Castle* is to represent the power and prestige of the Castle and the extent of its influence in the village.

ENEMIES

Kafka's heroes have enemies whose hostility is based on their own "personal" decision. Even in *Amerika* they are wholly committed to that world against which Karl must contend. They are in the service of injustice and of a disorder that has donned the semblance of order. So too are the officials who work for the Castle and the Law Court; but they remain "impersonal," always acting on instructions, in the pursuit of their duty, in accordance with some law—

never as individuals in their own right. In a word, they are mere functionaries.

To that extent the enemies appear to contradict what has just been said about the figures in Kafka's world—namely, that they are purely functionaries. But one feature, common to all these enemies, locates them firmly within that structured world again and vindicates them in their role as figures: their hostility towards the hero is always an absolute hostility. They have no *reason* to adopt a hostile attitude: they simply exist as expressions of hostility in its purest form.

The Anti-World and Its Representatives

In order to give an account of the hierarchies in *The Trial* and *The Castle,* we must begin by looking at their lowest ramifications. On one occasion in *Amerika* Kafka gives a description of an official that points forward to the later novels: the "senior hotel clerks" go about dressed in "black frock coats and top hats" (chap. 6). When the two employees of the Court come to take Joseph K. away for execution, they too are wearing frock coats and "top hats [that are] seemingly irremovable" (*The Trial,* last chapter). The officials and agents of authority who are visibly in evidence generally belong to the lower echelons. The descriptions that are given of these lower-placed officials conform to a more or less fixed pattern. Either they are inordinately slender and agile, like the first warder (*The Trial,* chap. 1), the Clerk of Inquiries (chap. 3) and Schwarzer (*The Castle,* chap. 1), in which case they are stylish, dressed always in tight-fitting clothes and generally theatrical in their manner; or else they are "fat," like the two executioners and the second warder. The black frock coats and top hats, which made their first appearance in *Amerika,* recur many times thereafter.

The higher the rank of an individual figure, the more sketchy is the description that can be given of him. The senior officials are virtually faceless. There is much uncertainty about their appearance, which actually alters according to their function. The image the villagers have of Klamm, for example, is "correct only in certain basic traits. . . . His appearance when he arrives in the village is said to be quite different from his appearance when he leaves . . . he looks different when he's alone, different again when he is talking to people, and when he is up at the Castle he is like a different person altogether—which is hardly surprising, all things considered" (chap.

16). This sentence shows why it is that whenever we speak of "characterization" we are only able to list a few isolated traits—the sort of thing that would be labelled "purely external" in the work of another writer. But let us recall once more Kafka's narrative technique: the story is told through the hero, who sees everything "only" from the outside. But what he sees, or rather the way he sees it, is all that there is to see; that in itself is sufficient as characterization. The example of Klamm makes the point very clearly: outward change, brought about by a change in function, embodies the whole essence of such a figure. Behind the outward appearance there is—nothing. Only one of these many functions and faces is accessible to K., and that is the one assumed by the official in his direct dealings with K. Above all else the officials display an extraordinary degree of nervous sensibility in their contacts with the various parties and hence with K. This extreme sensibility is not a psychological characteristic in the normal sense, but an expressive device aimed at underlining the total class distinction between the official and the party he is dealing with. The degree of sensitivity shown by the official is determined by his rank, so that each official is necessarily characterized and defined by the position he occupies within the hierarchy. Thus we are told by the secretary Bürgel, in *The Castle,* that the officials "are people who, by virtue of their work, are endowed with a quite extraordinary subtlety of feeling" (chap. 18).

If the degree of sensitivity is contingent upon rank, then it follows that an official who occupies a senior position must be even more remote from the parties (because these "parties"—and Kafka allows the term's legal connotations full play—offend the officials' sensitivity by their very existence). This is why we know so little about these senior officials, and why all kinds of legends and exaggerated stories have grown up around them; and this is also the reason why they exercise such a powerful hold over the parties.

Because these officials are merely steps in the "infinite hierarchy" (*The Trial,* chap. 7), they cannot have any opinions of their own, nor can they be depicted as personalities. Everything they say is part of the established stock-in-trade of the hierarchical organization to which they belong. Consequently Kafka's figures have no past: this is a dimension that can properly be attributed only to the organization itself.

Although it is impossible to know exactly where these figures stand within the hierarchy of the structured world, they are always adequately defined by their function in relation to Kafka's heroes. Thus the landlady enlightens K. about Momus in these terms: "I'm not talking about him as a private person, but as he is when he acts with Klamm's assent . . . then he's a tool to be used by Klamm." (*The Castle,* chap. 9). And it is with this "tool," this mere creature, that K. has to conduct his business! As we have noted many times before, these tools of the authorities have their own very specific and characteristic patterns of gesture and movement. Thus the "enemies" are agile, quick and given to unexpected moves; the "companions" are clumsy, and apt to dash about restlessly in all directions; the defendants and villagers are recognizable by their stoop, and by the way they push and shove in a cowed mass, whispering among themselves; the emissaries of the organization are theatrical, smooth and stylish, or else fat and greasy; and the officials are defensive, timid, sensitive and suspicious. As we have also indicated before, these patterns of gesture and movement derive from the particular functions which these figures perform. Their physical being is determined by their role vis-à-vis the hero, whether it be to confuse him, disturb him, torment him, or simply let him flounder about in the dark. It is quite obvious that no such differences exist between real human beings; and that such a view of man cannot be encompassed by any empirical approach to human existence, in terms of anthropological, biological and psychological factors. Kafka devises new resources of expression to meet his particular needs.

REIFICATION

Kafka shifts the dividing line between the living and the inanimate in a direction that runs totally counter to the laws of nature—and all in the service of his expressive purpose. Thus he can write of a character that he looks "like a pole that's dangling about," or is "cut out of tissue paper," so that people can hear him "rustling" as he walks along. These figures make no sound when they laugh (*The Castle,* chaps. 7 and 15), and instead of coming of their own accord they are "placed in position" like objects (chap. 18). . . .

This process of depersonalization goes even further, to the point where some of Kafka's figures manipulate their own limbs and facial features, as if these were not naturally part of themselves but had somehow been presented to them as an afterthought for their use and entertainment. They are themselves surprised, annoyed and amused by all the different things they can do with them. They command their limbs by "tapping" them, as though not yet altogether sure of them—as though they might still take on a life of their own.

Everything that is normally contingent upon a personal consciousness capable of perceiving, enquiring and initiating action, or else upon the operation of certain laws of nature, has here taken on an independent existence of its own and become an object to be looked at and observed. When the warder is being beaten he does not cry out like a human being, but like "some tortured musical instrument," and the cry he utters is a sound "without pause or modulation" (*The Trial,* chap. 5). In other words, Kafka has depersonalized both the person and his form of utterance. All the things that normally exist in a state of flux—breathing, light, sound, pleasure, etc.—are arrested and held fast by Kafka, who renders them as tangible *objects*. As he himself says [in a passage omitted from *The Castle*], one must have the strength "to keep on staring at things without closing one's eyes . . . but if one relaxes for a single moment and closes one's eyes, then everything promptly dissolves into darkness."

HEARINGS AND EXAMINATIONS

The normal judicial process presupposes the existence of two parties and a third impartial authority, whose task it is to reach a judgment following the hearing. In Kafka's novels one of the two parties is the hero, who is invariably alone (except for one or two minor occasions in *Amerika*). He is defendant or plaintiff (a rigid distinction between the two is not always made), defending counsel and witness, all in one person. The other party is the world of organized disorder—or seeming order—in *Amerika*; the Court in *The Trial*; and the Castle itself, with all its ramifications, in *The Castle*. But the third element is missing: there is no impartial authority to sit in judgment. Judgment has been usurped by those who oppose the hero.

Such is the outcome of all these examinations and hearings: the two K.'s wear themselves out precisely because they encounter no real resistance. Their efforts are of no avail because their opponents, being in effect invisible, present them with no targets to hit. Their arguments are nullified by the sheer impenetrability of the mysterious systems that confront them. In the two main novels these hearings and examinations never result in a judgment. True, the two K.'s are notified of certain disadvantages in which they have now been placed, but nothing ever happens as a direct result of any negative outcome of such a hearing. It is left to the two heroes to form their own judgments and to pass judgment on themselves. This much is clear already: the opposition attaches no importance to these examinations; they are conducted solely in the interests of the two K.'s and the other parties. Up at the Castle they say that the various comings and goings of the parties serve no purpose except to "leave dirt all over the front-door steps [of the Herrenhof]" (chap. 17).

Discussions and Enquiries

The two K.'s always have to argue their case in person: they need to be physically present the whole time. For them there is no respite from a task that demands all their strength, whereas the opposing order can draw on a limitless fund of set formulas and traditions; the procedures they adopt against the two K.'s follow an established pattern that is virtually second nature to them, so that no particular effort is needed on their part. In fact it is not even necessary for the opposing order to encounter the heroes in the person of an agent or representative: it exists, and that is sufficient. The two K.'s wear themselves down in their struggle against an order that never actually shows its face. When, for example, K. has those interminable conversations with Olga about whether or not Barnabas is really employed on Castle business, or whether or not Klamm is really Klamm, he is unable to gain any insight at all into the "inextricable complexity" of the authorities "up there" (*The Castle,* chap. 15). The principle of negation is inherent in the very nature of the Castle. Every statement automatically elicits a statement to the contrary, its own suspension.

How Events Occur in Kafka's Novels

An episode is invariably set in motion by a *disturbance* of some kind. . . . The disturbance initiates the episode by alarming the opposing order—summoning it to the scene—and thereby setting in motion all that must inevitably follow. In every instance it is the heroes who are responsible for the disturbance. They force the opposing world to concern itself with them; and that is enough to make them guilty in the eyes of that world. The "burden of proof" for justifying the disturbance is placed firmly on their shoulders. When we use the term "disturbance," we are of course looking at things from the point of view of the opposing order. The two K.'s, however, see things very differently: to them this is no "disturbance," but the affirmation, no less, of their own existence. The implication is that if they were to back down and cease their disturbance—as the opposing order requires them to do—they would thereby nullify their own existence; but since what they seek is precisely to affirm that existence, they "disturb" the authorities. The opposing world then proceeds to nullify this disturbance in the manner already indicated: the fact that it thereby nullifies the existence of the two K.'s is unintended, in a sense it is a mere by-product of its primary purpose.

The act of nullification is the caesura that marks the end of the episode. This is the characteristic variable of Kafka's prose, its basic formal unit; and the work as a whole is the sum of countless variations on this one formal theme.

RHYTHM AND INFINITY

The Court maintains that it is only drawn towards the guilty: yet it *is* drawn towards Joseph K. It follows, therefore, that any attempt by K. to establish his innocence (and thus in a sense to prevent the trial from really getting under way) must constitute an act against the Court, and a disruption of its order. All the other defendants submit; Joseph K. alone creates a disturbance, and for this reason his efforts must be nullified.

The action of the trial unfolds in three parallel sequences: in the scenes at K.'s lodgings, at the bank and at the premises of the Court. No summary can hope to do more than suggest how some of these strands are developed, because the construction of this novel—unlike that of the earlier *Amerika*—runs on in an unbroken continuity throughout. The three strands are interwoven in complex fashion: one strenuous undertaking [to attain justification] issues into another, just as each act of nullification is followed in due course by another. Lodging-house, Court-room or bank—it really makes no difference where the action is taken up, since the figures in the novel function in exactly the same way wherever they are placed. The pace and rhythm of these episodes is rapid, hard and insistent. There are no pauses, no digressions and no possibilities of escape. The confrontation between the two orders is not interrupted by any long passages of description, in which K., like Karl in *Amerika,* might have been relegated to the role of spectator: on the contrary, K. cannot get away from his case—it is with him wherever he goes. When he walks down the street, people at their windows laugh at him; when he is sitting in his office thinking about his case, the Assistant Manager comes in, laughing out loud; and when he gets home in the evening, he thinks he sees a guard standing outside the house. His whole thinking is a sustained attempt to affirm his own existence—an attempt which is automatically nullified by the episodes incorporated in the action. And of course there are none of those turns for the better which helped to create the long narrative interludes in *Amerika.*

[Having considered the ending of *The Trial,*] let us now ask how *The Castle* might have ended. K.'s goal is to become indistinguishable from the villagers. If he were to achieve this goal, *The Castle* would be a novel in the strict sense of the word. The way that led from his arrival in the village to his final acceptance as a member of the community would be a journey, a progression, whose course would be charted through the gradual unfolding of the action. But it is surely clear all along that K. and the opposing order are so utterly different in kind that any hope of assimilation must be ruled out altogether. The novel does not in fact "develop" at all. It simply shows us the unfolding of a relationship whose pattern is implicit right from the first page. The more clearly this relationship between the two orders emerges, the more impossible it is for K. to become indistinguishable from the representatives of this opposing order, and the more clearly his position as an outsider is revealed.

Camus sees the conflict between the two opposing orders as a "living equation"; and the image is a useful one. However, K. is not the "x" of this equation, as Camus supposes, but a very precise quantity. The two terms of the equation are the Castle (= the quantity that annuls) and K. (= the quantity that affirms); and its value is "infinite." The two quantities are incommensurable: the only possible relationship between them is an absurd one. (Camus illustrates the point well by quoting the joke about the madman trying to catch fish in his bathtub, who carries on fishing even though he knows that "nothing will come of it.") Defining the absurd in an essay on "Philosophical Suicide," Camus writes that the degree of absurdity "will be progressively greater as the things I am comparing become more disparate."

If we apply this to Kafka and *The Castle,* then we must conclude that the gulf separating "eagle" from "slow-worm" (chap. 4) can never be bridged—not unless K. surrenders his very existence; and this he cannot do, since he has been put into the novel precisely in order to affirm his existence. Such a relationship is the very opposite of an "ultimate cause": it is an "absurd" relationship, which abolishes time and the possibility of progress, and exists suspended in a realm of undisturbed infinity, even if this means that in its outward form the work remains necessarily a fragment.

Chronology

1883	Franz Kafka born in Prague, July 3, to Hermann and Julie Löwy Kafka. Hermann, son of a Czech-Jewish country butcher's family, has risen, with the help of his wife's family, to establish his own business selling fancy goods. Franz's two brothers, born 1885 and 1887, both die in infancy. Three sisters, born 1889, 1890, 1892, later die in Nazi concentration camps.
1889–1901	Franz attends German elementary school and German Staatsgymnasium.
1901–06	Studies law at the German Karl-Ferdinand University in Prague.
1902	Meets Max Brod.
1905	Spends several weeks at a sanatorium, the first of many such stays, owing to chronic ill-health.
1906	Starts working in a law office as a secretary. Receives law degree. Embarks on his year of practical training in Prague law courts.
1907	Takes position with an insurance company, but complains that the long hours interfere with his writing.
1908	Eight prose pieces published under the title *Betrachtung* (*Meditation*). Accepts position with Workers' Accident Insurance Institute.
1909	Two sketches (originally part of "Description of a Struggle") published. Trip to Riva and Brescia (with Max and Otto Brod). "Die Aeroplane in Brescia" published.
1910	Five prose pieces published under the title *Betrachtung* (*Meditation*). Starts diary. Trip to Paris (with Max and Otto Brod). Visit to Berlin.

1911   Official trip to Bohemia. Trip (with Max Brod) to Switzerland, Italy, and France, writing travelogues. Becomes interested in Yiddish theater and literature. His family starts an asbestos factory, in which he is reluctantly involved at various times.

1912   Visits Leipzig and Weimar (with Max Brod). Meets Felice Bauer. *Meditation* published.

1913   "The Stoker" published (first chapter of work-in-progress *Amerika*). Visits Felice Bauer in Berlin. "The Judgment" published. Travels to Vienna and Italy.

1914   Engagement to Felice Bauer. Breaks off engagement. Visits Germany. Starts *The Trial*. Writes "In the Penal Colony."

1915   Reconciliation with Felice Bauer. *The Metamorphosis* published.

1916   Resumes writing after two years' silence: the fragments of "The Hunter Gracchus," "A Country Doctor," and other stories later included in *A Country Doctor*.

1917   Reengagement to Felice Bauer. Tuberculosis diagnosed. Takes extended sick leave. Engagement to Felice Bauer broken off again.

1918   Continued ill health. Intermittent stays at sanatoria.

1919   Brief engagement to Julie Wohryzek. "In the Penal Colony" and *A Country Doctor* (collection of stories) published. Writes "Letter to His Father."

1920   Begins correspondence with Milena Jesenská. Intermittent stays at sanatoria.

1921   After eight months of sick leave, goes back to work with the Workers' Accident Insurance Institute but has to take another leave two months later. "The Bucket Rider" published.

1922   Writes *The Castle,* "A Hunger Artist," "Investigations of a Dog." Breaks off relations with Milena Jesenská. Retires from Workers' Accident Insurance Institute. "A Hunger Artist" published.

1923   Meets Dora Dymant. Goes to live with Dora Dymant in Berlin.

1924   Moves back to Prague and then to Sanatorium Wiener Wald near Vienna. Dies at Sanatorium Kierling also near Vienna. Buried in Prague. Collection *A Hunger Artist* published shortly after his death.

Contributors

HAROLD BLOOM, Sterling Professor of the Humanities at Yale University, is the author of *The Anxiety of Influence, Poetry and Repression*, and many other volumes of literary criticism. His forthcoming study, *Freud: Transference and Authority*, attempts a full-scale reading of all of Freud's major writings. A MacArthur Prize Fellow, he is the general editor of five series of literary criticism published by Chelsea House. During 1987–88, he was appointed Charles Eliot Norton Professor of Poetry at Harvard University.

MAURICE BLANCHOT was called "the most eminent literary and cultural critic in France" by Paul de Man. Besides numerous novels, his works include *Faux Pas, Lautréamont et Sade, La Part du feu, Le Livre à venir*, and *L'Entretien infini*.

HEINZ POLITZER taught German Literature at Bryn Mawr, Oberlin, Cornell University and the University of California. He has published several books in German as well as articles on German and comparative literature. His full-length study of Kafka is called *Franz Kafka: Parable and Paradox*.

R. G. COLLINS teaches in the Department of English at the University of Ottawa.

A. E. DYSON, distinguished English critic, wrote *Yeats, Eliot, and R. S. Thomas, The Crazy Fabric: Essays in Irony,* and *The Inimitable Dickens: A Reading of the Novels*.

WALTER H. SOKEL is the Commonwealth Professor of German and English Literature at the Center for Advanced Studies at the University of Virginia. Besides articles on Kafka, he has written *The*

Writer in Extremis and *Franz Kafka: Tragik und Ironie* and edited an anthology of German Expressionist drama.

David I. Grossvogel, Goldwin Smith Professor of Comparative Literature and Romance Studies at Cornell University, is founder and editor of *Diacritics*. His books include *Divided We Stand, Twentieth-Century French Drama, Limits of the Novel,* and *Mystery and Its Fictions.*

Martin Walser is among the most prolific novelists in contemporary West Germany. His books include *Ehen in Philippsburg, Das Einhorn, Halbzeit.* His doctoral dissertation, *Beschreibung einer Form: Versuch über Franz Kafka,* was published in 1961.

Bibliography

Berman, Russell A. "Producing the Reader: Kafka and the Modernist Organization of Reception." *Newsletter of the Kafka Society of America* 6, nos. 1–2 (June–December 1982): 14–18.

Brod, Max. *Kafka: A Biography*. New York: Schocken, 1947.

Camus, Albert. *The Myth of Sisyphus*. New York: Knopf, 1955.

Canetti, Elias. *Kafka's Other Trial: The Letters to Felice*. New York: Schocken, 1974.

Deleuze, Gilles, and Félix Guattari. *Kafka: Toward a Minor Literature*. Minneapolis: University of Minnesota Press, 1986.

Dodd, W. J. "Varieties of Influence: On Kafka's Indebtedness to Dostoevski." *Journal of European Studies* 14, no. 4 (December 1984): 257–69.

Dolozel, Lubomir. "Intentional Function, Invisible Worlds, and Franz Kafka." *Style* 17, no. 2 (1983): 120–41.

Emrich, Wilhelm. *Franz Kafka: A Critical Study of His Writings*. New York: Ungar, 1968.

Feuerlicht, Ignace. "Kafka's Chaplain." *The German Quarterly* 39 (1966): 208–20.

Flores, Angel, ed. *The Kafka Debate*. New York: Gordian Press, 1977.

———, ed. *The Kafka Problem*. New York: Octagon, 1963.

Flores, Angel, and Homer Swander, eds. *Franz Kafka Today*. Madison: University of Wisconsin Press, 1962.

Gray, Ronald, ed. *Kafka*. Englewood Cliffs, N.J.: Prentice-Hall, 1962.

Greenberg, Martin. *The Terror of Art: Kafka and Modern Literature*. New York: Basic Books, 1965.

Hamburger, Michael. *A Proliferation of Prophets: Essays on German Writers from Nietzsche to Brecht*. Manchester: Carcanet Press, 1983.

Heller, Erich. *The Disinherited Mind: Essays on Modern German Literature and Thought*. New York: Harcourt Brace Jovanovich, 1975.

Hobson, Irmgard. "The Kafka Problem Compounded: Trial and Judgment in English." *Modern Fiction Studies* 23 (1977–78): 511–29.

Hughes, Kenneth, ed. *Franz Kafka: An Anthology of Marxist Criticism*. Hanover, N.H.: University Press of New England, 1981.

Kartiganer, Donald M. "Job and Joseph K.: Myth in Kafka's *The Trial*." *Modern Fiction Studies* 8 (1962): 31–43.

Kontje, Todd. "The Reader as Josef K." *The Germanic Review* 54 (1979): 62–66.

Krieger, Murray. *The Tragic Vision: Variations on a Theme in Literary Interpretation*. New York: Holt, Rinehart & Winston, 1960.

Leopold, Keith. "Breaks in Perspective in Kafka's 'Der Prozess.' " *The German Quarterly* 36 (1963): 31–38.

Mayo, Bruce. "Interpreting Kafka's Hidden Laughter." *The Germanic Review* 53 (1978): 166–73.

Modern Fiction Studies 8 (1962). Special Franz Kafka issue.

Mosaic 3, no. 4 (1970). Special Franz Kafka issue.

Politzer, Heinz. *Franz Kafka: Parable and Paradox*. Rev. ed. Ithaca: Cornell University Press, 1966.

Reed, Eugene E. "Franz Kafka: Possession and Being." *Monatshefte* 50 (1958): 359–66.

———. "Moral Polarity in Kafka's 'Der Prozess' and 'Das Schloss.' " *Monatshefte* 44 (1954): 317–24.

Reiss, Hans. *The Writer's Task from Nietzsche to Brecht*. London: Macmillan, 1978.

Rolleston, James. *Kafka's Narrative Theater*. University Park, N.Y.: Columbia University Press, 1974.

Seltzer, Alvin J. "Waking into Nightmare: Dream as Reality in Kafka's *The Trial*." In *Chaos in the Novel*. New York: Schocken, 1974.

Spilka, Mark. *Dickens and Kafka: A Mutual Interpretation*. Bloomington: Indiana University Press, 1963.

Stern, J. P. *The World of Franz Kafka*. London: Weidenfeld, 1980.

Strelka, Joseph. "Kafkaesque Elements in Kafka's Novels and in Contemporary Narrative Prose." *Comparative Literature Studies* 21 (1984): 434–44.

Sussman, Henry. "The Court as Text: Inversion, Supplanting, and Derangement in Kafka's 'Der Prozess.' " *PMLA* 92 (1977): 41–55.

Szanto, George L. *Narrative Consciousness: Structure and Perception in the Fiction of Kafka, Beckett, and Robbe-Grillet*. Austin: University of Texas Press, 1972.

Ziolkowski, Theodore. *Dimensions of the Modern Novel: German Texts and European Contexts*. Princeton: Princeton University Press, 1969.

Zyla, Wolodymyr T., ed. *Proceedings of the Comparative Literature Symposium: "Franz Kafka: His Place in World Literature" IV*. Lubbock: Texas Tech Press, 1971.

Acknowledgments

"The Work's Space and Its Demand" by Maurice Blanchot from *The Space of Literature* by Maurice Blanchot, translated by Ann Smock, © 1955 by Editions Gallimard, © 1982 by the University of Nebraska Press. Reprinted by permission of the University of Nebraska Press.

"Franz Kafka's Language" by Heinz Politzer from *Modern Fiction Studies* 8, no. 1 (Spring 1962), © 1962 by the Purdue Research Foundation, West Lafayette, Indiana. Reprinted by permission.

"Kafka's Special Methods of Thinking" by R. G. Collins from *Mosaic* 3, no. 4 (Summer 1970), Special Issue: *New Views on Franz Kafka.* © 1970 by the University of Manitoba Press. Reprinted by permission.

"Trial by Enigma: Kafka's *The Trial*" by A. E. Dyson from *Between Two Worlds: Aspects of Literary Form* by A. E. Dyson, © 1972 by A. E. Dyson. Reprinted by permission of St. Martin's Press, Inc. and Macmillan Press, London and Basingstoke.

"The Three Endings of Josef K. and the Role of Art in *The Trial*" by Walter H. Sokel from *The Kafka Debate: New Perspectives for Our Time,* edited by Angel Flores, © 1977 by Angel Flores. Reprinted by permission of The Gordian Press, Inc.

"*The Trial:* Structure as Mystery" (originally entitled "Kafka: Structure as Mystery") by David I. Grossvogel from *Mystery and Its Fictions* by David I. Grossvogel, © 1979 by The John Hopkins University Press, Baltimore/London. Reprinted by permission of The John Hopkins University Press.

"On Kafka's Novels" by Martin Walser from *The World of Franz Kafka,* edited by J. P. Stern, © 1980 by George Weidenfeld & Nicolson Ltd. Reprinted by permission of George Weidenfeld & Nicolson Ltd.

Index